W9-AND-084

Contents

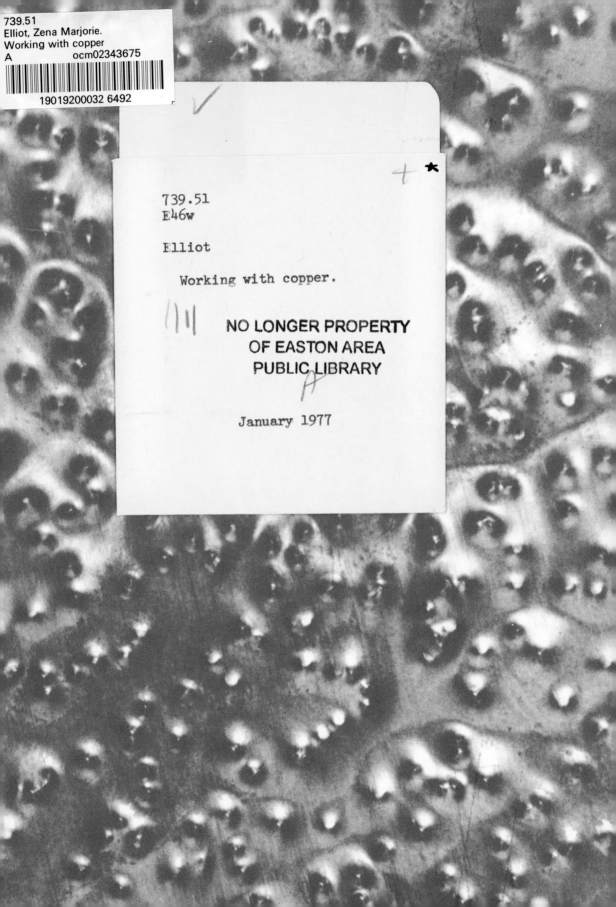

WORKING WITH
Copper

WORKING WITH
Copper

DRAKE

Published in 1976 by
Drake Publishers Inc.
801 Second Ave.
New York, N.Y. 10017

Copyright 1976 by Ure Smith
All Rights Reserved

ISBN: 0-8473-1078-7
LC: 76-1344

Printed in Hong Kong

Introduction

While I do not profess to know everything there is to know about the many and varied aspects of working with copper, in the years that I have been involved with it I have found, mostly by trial and error, a lot of workable angles and a significant lack of available easy-to-follow instructions in book form. Also a reluctance on the part of established copper workers to share the secrets of their success.

To off-set the impersonal perfection of this computerized space-age, people, whether adults or children, have an inherent need to return to creative self-expression. The aesthetic appeal and therapeutic value of 'doing your own thing' is enormous whether purely for pleasure, as a major work for a public examination, or as a paying hobby. However, a little guidance in the correct method of tackling a project will save a lot of disappointment.

The result is this book in which I have attempted to explain, by means of photos, diagrams and simple instructions, a wide variety of techniques for those already gripped by 'copper-fever' and those who would like to be if they knew how and where to start.

Zena Elliot

From here to antiquity

Copper is believed to be the first metal worked by man, understood and exploited at a very early stage of civilization. The fact that it was extensively used in the pure state is proved by the discovery of dishes and nails in the burial chambers of Ur and Erech dating from the third millenium B.C., and copper buckles and weapons in the palaces of Nineveh. Some pieces of copper and copper axes which have been found in the ruined cities of the Chaldean and Sumerian civilizations, may possibly date from as early as 4000 B.C.

Many copper mines were in operation in early times, for example during the eighteenth dynasty (circa 1580-1322 B.C.) in Egypt. Ancient Greeks mined their copper on the island of Eurobea and used it extensively for weapons and household utensils until about 900 B.C. The Romans obtained their copper from various provinces of their empire, notably Hespania Bailica in Spain and the Phoenician mines in Ituelva. Also in Germania from about 300 B.C. onwards, where discoveries of tools and utensils from this period show skilled Teutonic craftsmanship. Hungary also began mining copper in Roman times, while many other countries were to become important sources of supply in later centuries.

Each successive civilization — Arabian, Byzantine, Renaissance Italy — encouraged the art of working copper. Skills, many of which originated with the Sumerians and Egyptians, were handed down from craftsmen to apprentices and tools and techniques were gradually developed and perfected. This is understandable as apart from an attractive reddish colour, copper is soft, malleable and ductile which makes it easy to work but it can be hardened by hammering. As copper conducts heat well it is well suited for cooking utensils, especially since it was discovered in antiquity that tinning the interiors stopped food contamination. It can be polished to a warm attractive glow.

In time the popularity of copper was superseded by bronze, an alloy of copper and tin, which is very hard and which therefore had a wider variety of uses, the main advantage being that it can be cast. It was popularized by the Phoenicians from the second century B.C. as their ships plied a trade the length and breadth of the Mediterranean consisting of 90 per cent copper and 10 per cent tin. Bronze in turn gave way to iron, but neither of these metals possesses the ductility of copper and imposes limitations on craftsmen. Pure copper and brass — an alloy of copper and zinc first used on a large scale by the Romans — have remained the most popular choice for decorative metal-work right through the ages. Copper gilding (made of 5 parts copper to 1 part zinc) also enjoyed great favour over many centuries.

During the late seventeenth and eighteenth centuries copper enjoyed a second period of popularity and again during the twentieth century. However over the last ten years it has become more and more a way of life, and its uses in industrial, plumbing and electrical fields, building and home decoration are legion.

A world increasingly orientated to mass-produced, drip-dry, assembly-lined look-alike, throw-aways has

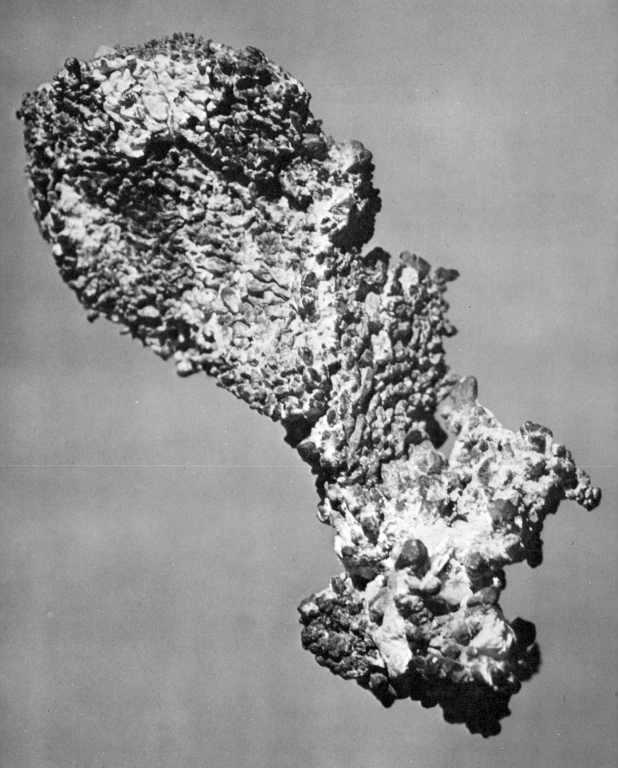

Copper ore.

created a demand for the individual touch and has caused a revival in folk art and handcrafted articles of all kinds. Copperwork is leading the field as all ages find it so easy and satisfying to work. It can be handled in so many different ways, to produce such a wide variety of articles that its appeal is endless for old and young, male and female, the part-time hobbyist or the dedicated craftsman and it finds a ready and fast growing market amongst those who have not the time or inclination to 'have a go' themselves but are ready and willing to join the cult of copper fanciers. Therefore copperwork can become a fascinating and paying pastime and can profitably fill many spare minutes or hours. The outlay is small and the return in terms of self-expression, satisfaction, sense of achievement and therapeutic value is beyond price. I would specially recommend it for anybody who has a physically or mentally exacting occupation, for those with a worried mind or anybody suffering from boredom. Once started you will become so involved that all other commitments pale into insignificance.

Do you know what you want?

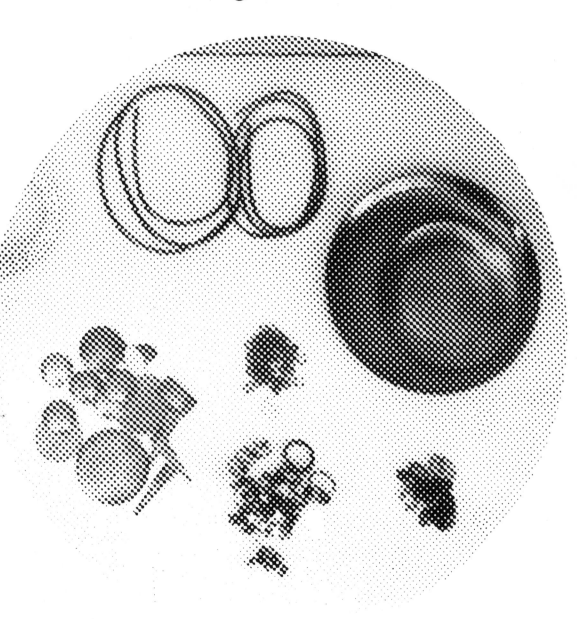

Copper can be easily bought in a wide variety of forms, already annealed (soft), half hard or hard. Knowing what you need for the job you have in mind saves time and trouble. Wires and rods are available either round or square in a variety of thicknesses and can be used to create elegant pieces of jewellery. For jewellery 20 gauge, 18 gauge, 16 gauge and 14 gauge will be most suitable — the higher the gauge number, the thinner the wire. Twelve gauge or heavier is called a rod and is more suitable for such things as wire sculptures and component parts of mobiles in the annealed form, or, bought as hard, are rigid rods for sculptural forms etc. The wire is soft and easily formed either by hand or with pliers, but after shaping can be textured and work-hardened by hammering. Excellent effects for heavier jewellery such as bracelets or belts, or wall sculptures can be obtained by twisting together 2 strands of the lighter gauge wires using a hand or electric drill as will be explained in the jewellery section.

Copper wire up to 30 gauge or even finer is available and can be knitted, crocheted, french-knitted or worked on a daisy wheel to make collars, chokers, evening bags and a wide variety of articles. Let your imagination have free rein after you get the feel of the material. The finer gauges are also used for stringing geometrical designs for plaques. Strip copper in 6 mm or 12 mm width is handy for cutting into lengths for rings or bracelets and can be simply shaped, etched or hammered. It is also an easy component for mobiles because the edges are already finished.

Sheet metal is also available in various gauges, graded the same way as the wire — for example, 12 gauge is very heavy, 28 gauge is very thin. Twelve—twenty gauge is most suitable for beaten articles, the heavier the gauge the easier it is to manage. Remember the thicker the copper is, the harder it is to cut and the more heat is needed to anneal it when it becomes work-hardened. Try to suit the gauge to the end result, a beaten tray needs to be fairly heavy and rigid, about 14-16 gauge; for a bowl, depending on the size, 16-18 gauge is sufficient. For double etched articles 20 gauge up to 28 gauge (for something of light appearance like butterflies' wings) is sufficient. Twenty-two gauge is good for an etched or beaten bracelet where weight is a consideration while 20 gauge is excellent for other etched articles such as a pendant or a coffee table top. If you decide to make a lidded box for instance the 12-14 gauge is easier to solder together. Turned bowls, plates of all sizes and shapes are readily available at most craft and hobby stores and can be etched or enamelled. These are 19 gauge and the blanks are also on sale in this gauge so that you can beat your own without needing to cut and finish the edge.

Most hobby shops also sell a very wide variety of ready-cut shapes for every conceivable kind of jewellery from an ear-ring to a large pendant, excellent for enamelling and with all the 'findings' (attachments for ear-rings, cuff links, rings, key rings, plus bracelet and necklace links and catches, jump rings etc.) that you could possibly require. If cutting your

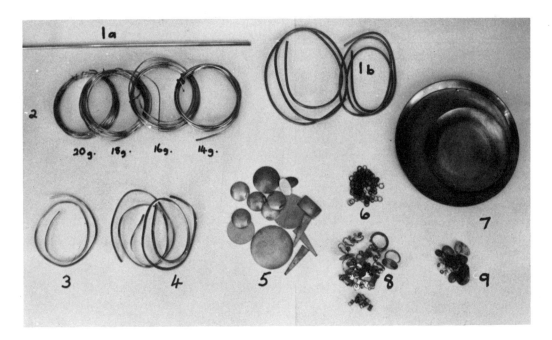

USEFUL MATERIALS FOR COPPERCRAFT

1a   *Copper rod, half hard, for wall sculptures, mobiles.*

1b   *8g., 10g. copper rod, soft, for heavy work but easily bent.*

2   *20-14 gauge copper wire, soft, can be coiled, twisted together, made into chains, used in an endless variety of ways.*

3   *Half round 12g., soft, good for motifs on jewellery, etc., can be bent with pliers.*

4   *Square wire, soft, can be attractive with hammered texture after shapes are made.*

5   *18g. copper blanks for jewellery, enamelling, etching or overlay with patterns in copper or brass.*

6   *Jump rings, two sizes, for joining.*

7   *19g. spun dishes for enamelling or etching, available in all sizes and shapes.*

8   *Findings (i.e. backings for cuff-links and rings, attachments for ear-rings, key rings, etc.).*

9   *Variety of stones, real and synthetic.*

own jewellery shapes for enamelling 18 gauge would be best and they have pieces of all gauges for sale.

They supply everything for the hobbyist from tools to enamelling requirements, stones for setting, ready made chains, and at a reasonable cost.

Copper shim is also sold there, in lengths up to 1.85 m. For really large quantities however, contact a metal merchant. Copper shim is a soft, workable, thin copper and can be mounted and used for decorative tiles, plaques, feature walls, door panels, lamp bases and an endless variety of things. It is cut with scissors and can even be woven in strips into lamp shades. (See page 28.)

Opposite:
Two examples of backed copper shim. (For step-by-step instructions see page 25.) Left: heat colouring, right: coppertone.

Overleaf:
A woven copper T.V. lamp made from copper shim and a pair of wooden embroidery frames. (See page 28 for instructions.)

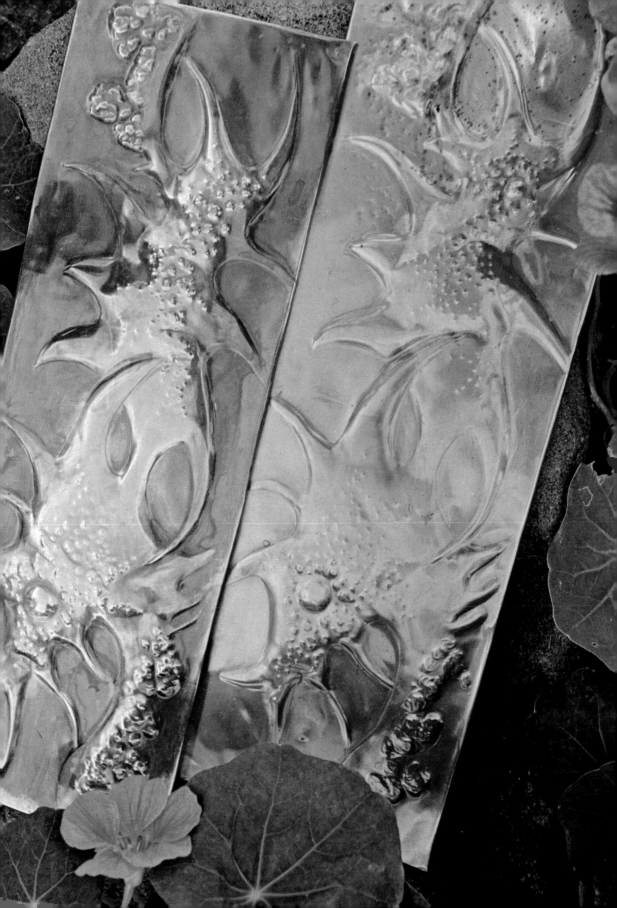

The importance of design

Going right back through civilization to pre-historic times, we find that design is related to human needs. Every era has produced its own interpretation of nature and a life style which is relevant to that time. When pre-historic man decorated his cave walls with crude drawings of bison and other animals, he was not consciously designing something, he was acting out the day's hunt, psychologically giving himself courage as he drove his wooden spears into the image he had created. This magic rite was important to his survival, without food he could not exist. Similarly, the earliest little sculptured figures were fertility symbols, fertility of the animals (food) and of themselves (to build up strength in numbers) was of vital importance to them. Before man learned to make his own clothes he had found ways to decorate his body, with daubs of clay, feathers in his hair, with patterns drawn on his skin with a burnt stick. This gave him pleasure and satisfied a basic psychological urge which is still strongly apparent in even the most advanced society today. Self adornment in the form of jewellery and clothing for modern man keeps many hundreds of thousands of designers gainfully employed.

The emphasis today is on form (shape) as the important element in design. Everything is simplified, stream-lined, abstracted, but functional. There is beauty in uncluttered simplicity. We do not have time for the heavy ornate pomposity of the past, for example, the Victorian era. Accordingly, when designing your articles keep their line simple, clean and flowing. Look to nature for inspiration, that is where most designs originate, for example, the grain in knotty wood, pebbles, rock formation, seedpods, insect life, marine life, driftwood, plant forms and photographed enlargements of cells and crystals for a start will provide endless possibilities. Collect the actual articles as you discover them, or make little sketches for later reference and you will never lack for ideas.

For those individuals who swear they can't draw a straight line (and this is certainly a very hard thing to do without a ruler!), it is possible to cheat a little and still produce some very satisfying results. Look for an appealing design, not too fussy, that you feel relates to the article you have in mind, and enlarge it. For example, if you find a small design, about 7 x 10 cm and you wish to make a plaque 30 x 40 cm then the solution is simple. Mark in all round the edges for 6 mm and draw lines so that the design is covered in 6 mm squares. Draw out a 30 x 40 cm oblong on a sheet of drawing paper or butcher's paper, mark it off in 2 cm and draw the lines so you now have a 2 cm squared graph. For easy reference number crossways and downways on both the 6 mm and 2 cm graph, and by following the lines of the drawing on the original picture transfer them to the corresponding square on the larger one. Hey presto, you have reproduced a creditable drawing with the minimum effort!

For jewellery, go back in time to the Pre-Columbian or Aztec eras in South America and study the simplicity of their forms and figures and marvel at the workmanship of their crude tools.

Copper pendants.

Many of their motifs can be adapted
or reproduced with good effect on
modern bracelets and necklaces —
brass patterns on copper, or copper on
copper can look good, and enamelled
copper can be used either alone or
added to give colour to copper
jewellery pieces.

All primitive jewellery has
something to offer. From Peru,
Mexico, the North American Indian
or South African native tribes you will
find inspiration from nature suited to
their life style and adaptable to ours.
Having once got into your stride,
original ideas will come more easily.
Keep a box of bits and pieces, even
pieces you try and don't finish because
they fail to please you at the time can
often be reorganized into something
else at a later date.

Copper shim

.006 copper is available in 30 cm and 60 cm widths at most craft stores. While a variety of tools are now available, improvisation is cheaper and works just as well

Prepare a suitable design, using pencil, cut the shim with scissors allowing for turnings, secure drawing paper to surface with Scotch tape, and you are ready to begin.

for texturing.

3. Wooden spoon — if edges are square, round off with sandpaper. Use both the bowl and handle for pressing out design from the back. Place copper on a thick amount of wet newspaper for this.

4. Plastic bowl scraper — use on the right side of the design to flatten down background and neaten edges. Put on

TOOLS YOU WILL NEED

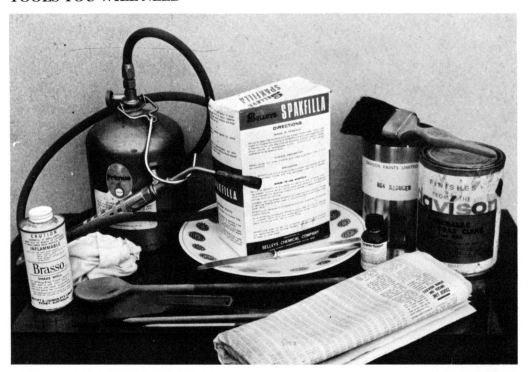

1. Biro — for drawing round the design so you can see where you have gone. (Place on a couple of sheets of newspaper so you get a deep impression.)

2. Meat skewer — smooth sharp point and blunt end with sandpaper and use as required for small areas of design or

a hard surface to do this.

5. Brasso for polishing.

6. Soft cloth. If using Coppertone to colour, polish both before and after, if heat colouring, polish only after copper has been filled and mounted.

7. Gas torch with smallest end fitting for heat colouring.

8, 9 and 10. Plaster of Paris for filling raised design, plate and knife for mixing.

11 and 12. 804 Reducer (thinners) and metal lacquer. Use half and half with a soft brush (13) to seal the finished article against tarnishing.

14. Coppertoner — easy to use colouring agent as an alternative to heat. One to two drops in half a cup of boiling water, applied with a small soft cloth after the job has been mounted, filled and polished. Allow to dry thoroughly then repolish highlights, and finish with lacquer. Gives bronze, green, purple and dark tones according to strength.

15. Quantity of newspaper — use two dry sheets under copper when putting on design, use a thick amount **wet** when working design to allow the copper to stretch.

16. Sheet of plate glass to put under shim when flattening the background on the right side. A smooth part of a desk top is a suitable substitute.

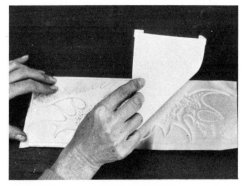

Step 2. Remove drawing — you should have a clear impression.

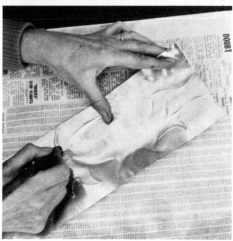

Steps 3 and 4. Turn upside-down on thick wet newspaper and begin to press the pattern out with the wooden spoon, bowl or handle according to size (or even skewer if very fine).

PATTERN COPPER SHIM
(see photograph on page 17).

Step 1. Tape design to copper shim, place on newspaper and draw round firmly with a biro.

Step 5. Turn right side up and flatten background with plastic bowl scraper (on glass or desk top). Do not proceed too far at a time before flattening background or the design will crease.

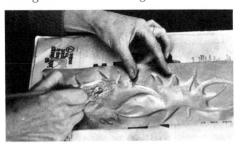

Step 6. Any extra raised parts of the design are done last — e.g. dots, spots, rigging on a ship etc.

Step 7. Turn right side up and neaten edges and background once more.

Step 8. Heat colour before filling. Place on fire bricks (or tripod and mesh if small). Rotate the tip of small blue flame over area to be coloured — the colours will spread but with practice can be fairly controlled. Do not overheat or fire scale, not colour, will result.

Step 9. Mix Plaster of Paris with water according to the instructions on packet.

Step 10. Fill raised pattern only, levelling with knife and scraping off background area. Allow to dry completely.

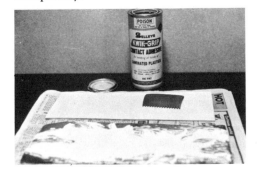

Step 11. Cut backing of stiff cardboard (for small article) or 5 mm marine ply (for large plaque) allowing for shim to turn over round edges.

Step 12. Spread contact cement on both surfaces.

Step 13. When touch dry join, press firmly together, fold over edges.

Step 14. Turn right side up and press all over to ensure a good contact.

Polish with Brasso and a soft cloth to remove colour where not desired and to raise highlights in design. If you want a stippled or tooled background, do it now. Small dots or lines can be added with the skewer, or larger ones with the round end of a ball pein hammer or a punch of any desired shape or pattern.
Note: If you wish the texturing to show up as part of the design rather than to disguise any blemishes in the background, do it before polishing, so that colour will remain in the depressions. Finish surface with lacquer and mount as desired.

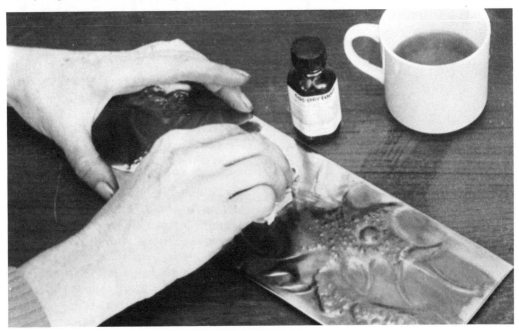

As an alternative to heat colouring Coppertoner can be used. Proceed through the working instructions omitting Step 8. When Step 14 has been completed polish well with Brasso finish and a clean cloth to remove any residue. Mix one or two drops of Coppertoner in half a cup of boiling water and rub over the surface quickly with a small soft cloth. Allow to dry completely before polishing with a soft cloth with or without Brasso according to the amount of highlights you desire. Wipe over with 804 thinners and apply metal lacquer (50-50 with thinners) with a soft brush, or spray if preferred.

WOVEN COPPER T.V. LAMP
(See photograph on page 18)

Requirements
A pair of wooden embroidery frames (diameter 22 cm); 2.30 m 3/8 by 5/8 wood for legs; a piece of 3 ply to cut three pronged base; light socket with switch, wire and plug; flat black spray paint; .006 gauge copper (shim) 30 cm x 67 cm; scrap strips of shim and pieces of wire.

Step 1. With pencil and ruler mark shim into 13 mm strips from 13 mm border along one 67 cm edge, keep the lines straight. At unequal distances divide some of the strips in half (6 mm wide) to give interest to the pattern. With a pair of scissors cut the strips as shown leaving the uncut edge.

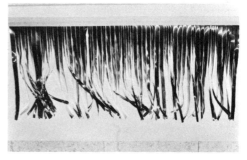

Step 2. On a piece of cardboard or 3 ply, draw out an oblong 30 x 67 cm. Some more guide lines can be added to help you keep the weaving straight. Lay the uncut edge along the top line and secure with masking tape.

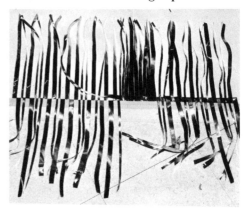

Step 3. Fold back every alternate strip, take another strip cut from scrap, secure one end with a small piece of masking tape and lie it along as close as possible to the top, folding down the raised strips as you go. When you have progressed about 15 cm start at the beginning to fold up the opposite strips to hold the horizontal strip firmly in place. When the row is completed make sure that the right hand vertical strip lies parallel to the drawn guide line then secure the end with another little piece of masking tape. The next horizontal strip is added under opposite verticals.

Step 4. Continue to add strips of varying widths in a woven pattern. The addition of some sections of soft wire will enhance the design. Continue until no more strips can be added, being careful to keep the weaving straight at all times.

Step 5. Secure all round with masking tape and spray with metal lacquer to prevent tarnishing.

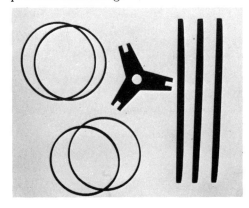

Step 6 (opposite column, bottom). Cut 3 46 cm legs and plane slightly on the top and bottom of one side only. Cut shape for base from 3 ply, spray these and embroidery rings with the flat black spray paint.

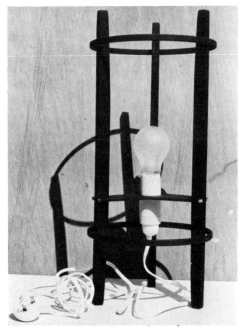

Step 7. Assemble base by tacking inside rings to legs and gluing in base.

Step 8. Glue woven copper to frame so that the overlap lines up with one of the legs, neaten with over-strip and screw to leg. Attach outer rings and secure with small screws.

Two methods of beating a copper bowl

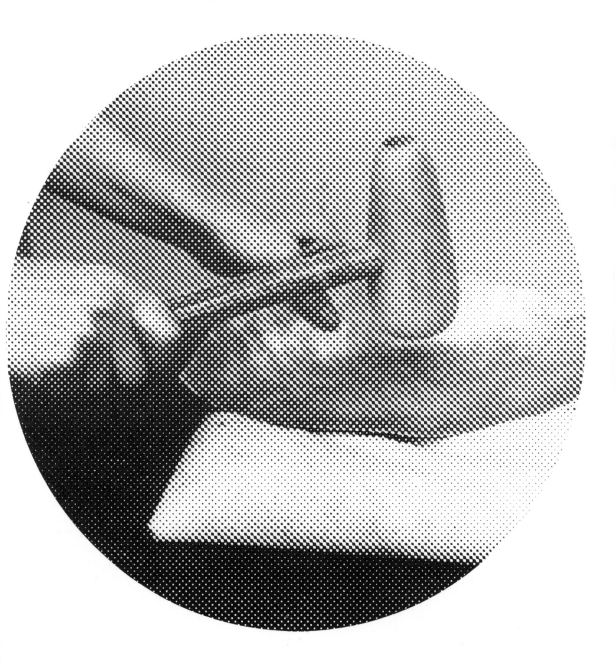

(See photograph on page 35.)

Implements for beating copper bowl

1. Using a recessed block — this can be made from a solid piece of wood such as an old table leg or the end of a cross-cut log. With your wire cutters make a circle of 20 gauge copper. (If desired, 18g. or 16g. can be used and is easier to work.) With a pair of compasses and a pencil, mark out several circles as a guide for beating. File the edge smooth using a large file followed by a small file and smooth with steel wool.

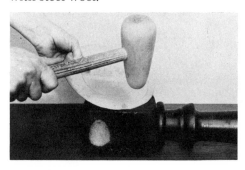

Step 1. Begin at the outer edge, holding at an angle over the recess, beat with the tapered end of a pear-shaped wooden mallet, rotating copper as you beat.

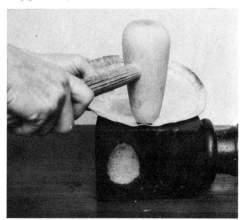

Step 2. As 'frills' develop on the edge, hold over the flat part of the block and hammer out.

Steps 3 and 4 (opposite and above). Continue to work in circles towards the centre, straightening the edge as necessary.

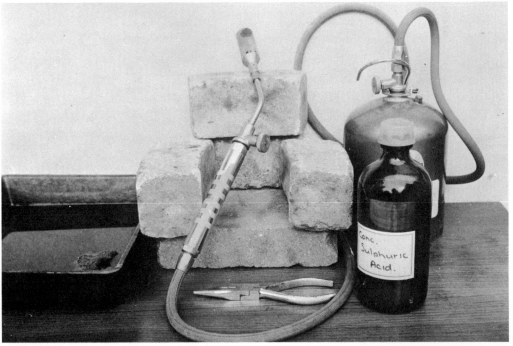

Step 5. When the copper becomes 'work-hardened' and is difficult to hammer it will need annealing. This requires a gas torch with a large end fitting, some fire bricks, pliers for lifting hot metal, a bucket of water for cooling and a dish of pickle (1 part concentrated sulphuric acid to 8-10 parts water). Remember, always **add acid to water** for cleaning.

Step 6. Place the copper on the fire bricks and heat until cherry red, rotating the flame.

Step 7. With the pliers transfer to the bucket of water.

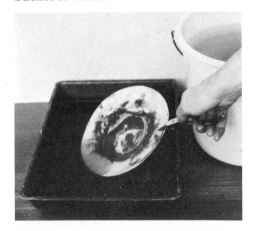

Step 8. Place in the pickle until copper turns pink.

Step 9. Clean off the fire scale with steel wool and rinse well, preferably under running water.

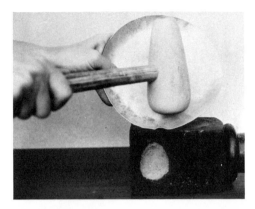

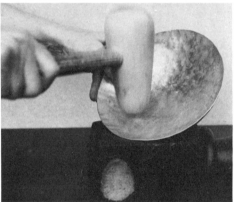

Steps 10, 11, 12. Beginning once more at the edge repeat the process of shaping, working in circles towards the centre and beating out 'frills' in the edge as they occur. Repeat annealing if necessary — finish by flattening bottom so dish will stand.

Polish and finish as previously described.

Simple copper bowls made from 20 gauge copper. An ideal exercise in elementary copper work. (See page 32 and 37 for instructions on the two methods of beating out copper bowls.)

2. Using a Sandbag — make a bag of calico, loosely fill with sand, and tie the neck securely. Cut a shape in 20g. (or thicker) copper as before, filing and smoothing the edge and marking some guide lines for beating.

Step 1 (below). Beginning at the outside edge, beat the copper into a concave shape working in rows as before. When 'frills' occur from beating, remove by beating onto a hard flat surface.

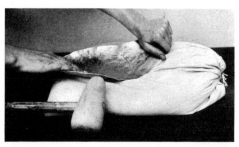

Step 2 (above). Anneal as before when work-hardened and straighten the shape while still soft.

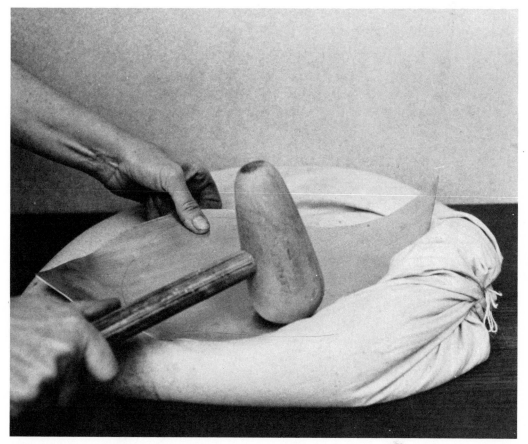

Copper pendants without solder, clockwise from the top: a 20 gauge copper pendant with an overlay of a brass design cut with a nibbler; an abstract setting for two stones, with 12 gauge wire shaped onto sheet copper; zodiac pendant with the sign of Aries beaten onto an antiqued copper shape; etched pendant (using the masking tape method) with stone setting; pendant of 6 mm rectangular copper section, and a free swinging shape in 12 gauge copper wire (See page 71 for instructions).

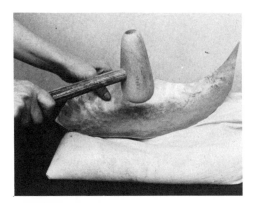

Step 3. Continue to beat until the copper is the desired depth.

Step 4. Shape the end as far as possible by beating over wood.

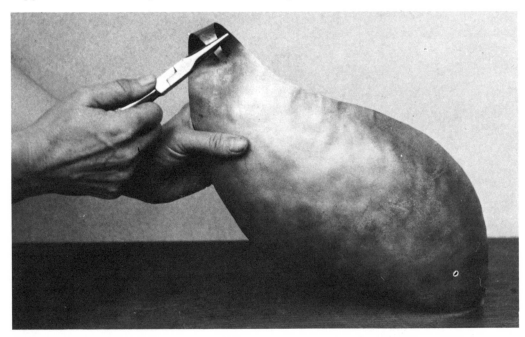

Step 5. Complete the curve with pliers. Polish and finish as desired.

Cleaning copper

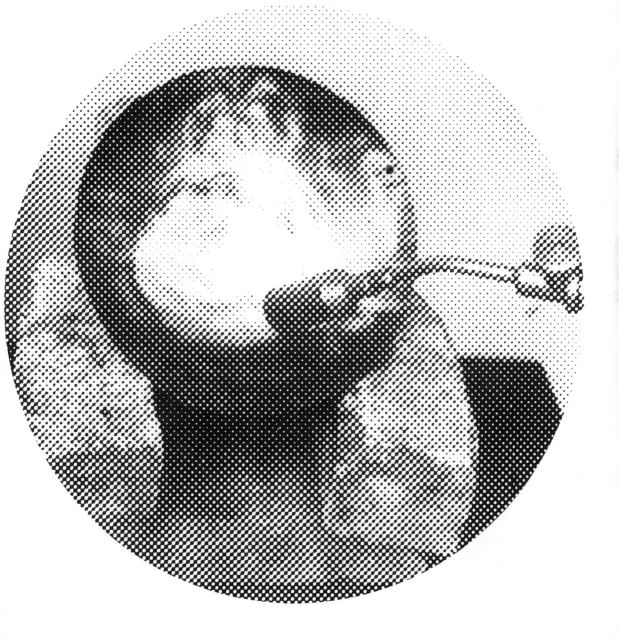

Copper can be cleaned in quite a variety of ways, depending on the job in hand. Sheet copper, blanks and turned articles, when bought, have a protective coating which must be removed along with the dirt that it attracts, before using it for such things as etching or enamelling.

Note: Regardless of which method you use always hold by the edges, **never** put fingers on the cleaned surface as more greasy marks will result.

CLEANING WITHOUT ACID

Vinegar and Salt — this is a safe, cheap and very useful method of cleaning, especially in a classroom. Add ¼ cup of cooking salt to half a litre of malt vinegar, white vinegar will do but brown is better. Shake well to blend and keep in a bottle when not in use. Pour into a bowl and use with steel wool or dobbie pad. Rinse well, preferably under running water.

Fine soap pads — rinse well.

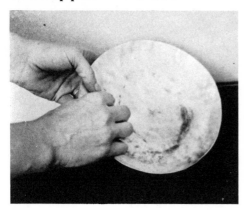

Detergent and fine steel wool.
steel wool.

Sparex 2 — a commercial preparation for cleaning copper, as effective as acid but safer, especially for children. Mix as directed, keep in a small lidded plastic bucket or screw top jar, 280 grams makes approximately one litre. It will keep indefinitely and can be used over and over again but store away from tools, steel cabinets etc., or they will rust. Use with dobbie pad, **never steel wool,** hold by the edges, and rinse thoroughly.

Apart from general cleaning it is excellent for removing fire scale especially from the back of enamelled pieces but in this case do not submerge, hold in the hand and clean the back only or the Sparex will dull the colours. For enamelling, which burns back from the edges or has bare spots, submerge and leave for a few minutes before cleaning, to make a good surface for re-enamelling.

Whiting and Ammonia — essential for cleaning etched copper plates for printing and also good for cleaning etched bowls after removing hand ground or block-out lacquer. Pour out a shallow dish of whiting and one of household ammonia. Dip a soft cloth into the ammonia and then into the whiting and rub hard on the surface of the copper. Rinse thoroughly.

Turpentine — a little turpentine on a soft cloth will remove sticky residue left by Scotch tape or masking tape.

Brasso — applied with a soft cloth and polished vigorously will clean copper, before applying lacquer always wipe over with thinners to remove any residue.

CLEANING WITH ACID

Warning — Always add the acid to the water, not vice versa, or it will spit and cause nasty burns. Use in a well-ventilated room preferably with a fan, do not inhale the fumes.

Pickle 1 part concentrated sulphuric acid or 1 part concentrated nitric acid to 8-10 parts water.

1. Measure water into a container, glass or heavy plastic, large enough to hold the articles to be cleaned (a lidded pyrex dish, a small lidded plastic bucket, or for larger articles a deep plastic tray or crisper from an old fridge will work well).
2. Add the acid gradually, stirring carefully with a wooden stick. Heat will be generated.

3. Carefully submerge the article to be cleaned so as not to splash the acid.
4. Leave until the copper turns pink.
5. Remove with wooden or copper tongs and hold under running water. Persistent fire scale can be removed from the surface with dobbie pad. If it will not all come free, return to the acid for a short time and rinse and clean again.

Pickle can be covered with a lid and re-used until it turns a fairly dark turquoise colour. When exhausted pour into a sink with freely flowing water to make a very diluted solution which will not damage drains.

Note: Never put copper into pickle while hot, cool it in water first.

HEAT CLEANING

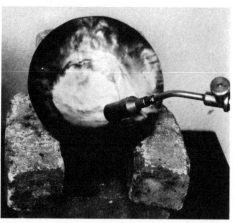

Place shape or bowl on a wire mesh and put it into a kiln until it glows faintly red. Remove, allow to cool slightly on an asbestos mat or pad, a metal surface or fine brick and then plunge into water, or heat similarly with the gas torch. With either method do not overheat or too much fire scale will be produced. After cooling in water put into pickle and clean with dobbie pad then rinse thoroughly.

BRIGHT DIP

Half concentrated sulphuric acid and half concentrated nitric acid, plus a pinch of common salt.

This is extremely dangerous to mix and to use. Every precaution must be taken. It generates a great deal of heat on combination and should be allowed to stand in a safe place for 24 hours before using.

With tongs, dip the metal in the solution and remove immediately, washing well under running water. Bright dip is used extensively in industry for cleaning both copper and brass articles, but it must be treated with a great deal of respect. It is completely unsuitable for use in a classroom, and if the idea frightens you it is best to leave it alone — nervousness leads to accidents.

Oxidizing and colouring

COPPERTONER

This is a commercial product for colouring copper.

One or two drops in half a cup of boiling water, rubbed on the surface (previously well polished with Brasso) with a small soft cloth gives a variety of colours, green, purple or black according to strength. Allow it to dry thoroughly before polishing with either a soft cloth or one dampened with Brasso according to how many highlights you want in the design.

Use on jewellery pieces, etched articles etc. after they have been completed and polished with Brasso. For articles like chains or coil jewellery which would be difficult to polish, dip in copper cleaner, rinse well and then dip into Coppertoner solution and hang up to dry before highlighting and finishing with lacquer.

For copper shim, complete design, fill and back, then polish well with Brasso. Apply Coppertoner (hot) with a small soft rag, wiping over the surface until the desired colour is achieved.

Do not allow puddles to form on the design. Dry thoroughly before polishing and finishing.

Note: Buy in small quantities as it goes a long way and will deteriorate with time. Even tightly capped it forms a white crust.

LIVER OF SULPHUR (sulphurated potash) is an oxidizing agent, available in lump form from most chemists and hobby shops. It must be kept airtight in a screw top jar. Dissolve in the proportion of a piece the size of an almond in 0.2 litres of boiling water. It must be used very hot but can be dissolved in a tin and kept over low heat on the stove or over a bunsen burner. Copper articles must be well polished with Brasso before oxidizing to remove the surface coating. While dipping is the most satisfactory method for jewellery, chains and small articles, such as bowls, it can be used on large pieces like plaques after they are filled and backed by pouring a little on the surface and rubbing over the design with steel wool. However, I have found from experience that it is better to polish shim of the required size for a plaque and oxidize in a large container, a stainless steel laundry trough, before working the design. The shim can be bent to submerge in the liquid or held by each end and dipped all over. Stand on one edge to dry so that the excess drains off, and work in the usual way, polishing with Brasso after the design has been finished, filled and backed.

Jewellery pieces should be allowed to dry thoroughly, then highlights raised with steel wool or Brasso before lacquering. Liver of Sulphur gives off hydrogen sulphide gas which not only smells unpleasant but is also poisonous, so use in a well ventilated area, preferably with a fan.

HEAT COLOURING

This is the method of colouring copper with carefully controlled heat using a gas torch with the smallest end fitting, a bunsen burner, or even by holding the copper over a gas ring with tongs, although this gives an overall colour instead of producing different colours in different areas of the design. It works very well on copper shim. You will find by experience that a little heating results in a deep bronze colour while further heating brings up purples and beautiful aqua greens. Keep the heat moving and don't overdo it or the colours will be lost and fire scale will be produced instead. The colour tends to spread but can be removed from unwanted areas with Brasso and a cloth over one finger, then polish the whole surface lightly.

Note: Do the heat colouring before filling the copper shim. It is then better to leave the polishing until the shape is filled and backed because too much enthusiastic rubbing could dent the design as the copper is softened.

Some people like to heat colour beaten bowls after the desired shape has been obtained. This involves careful heating without cooling in water or cleaning in pickle afterwards. It still softens the metal which must then be rehardened by beating. Because of the amount of heat needed if the copper is thick, a certain amount of fire scale will be unavoidable but adds dark colour, which is just lacquered over. While I don't personally care for the result, it does have appeal.

PATINAS

For those with some experience in the use of chemicals many different coloured patinas can be produced on copper. In particular, the green is a short-cut to the aged look seen on old copper steeples etc.

PAINT

While some people favour the addition of coloured lacquers and enamels to the backgrounds of their copper designs, I personally think that it cheapens the appearance and is quite alien to the nature of the material. While heat or chemicals reveal the colours within the metal, the addition of paint masks the beauty of the copper so why do it? If you want brilliant colour, the addition of enamel jewellery or enamelled shapes is far more desirable. Cast resin shapes

with added colour are also worthy of
consideration.

ENAMEL

Enamel, which is bought in a powder,
is basically a combination of clear
glass in the form of flux and metal
oxides which give the colour. It can be
obtained either in a transparent or
opaque form. Clear transparent flux
used in conjunction with the coloured
enamels gives more depth to the
appearance of transparent enamels
because used on copper the warm
shade of the metal shines through.

Enamelling simply means fusing a
layer or layers of this prepared powder
onto the surface of the copper with
heat. Many and varied effects can be
obtained by the use of ball and/or
thread enamels, metal foils etc. in
conjunction with the enamel powder.
For full instructions refer to the
chapter on Enamelling Techniques
(page 85).

Filling and backing copper shim

When working with copper shim, any design raised more than 3 mm must be filled in order to retain its form. There are several methods that can be used, depending on the size and the circumstances.

Copperfill wax — obtainable at most craft or hobby stores is suitable for small jobs.

Spakfilla (Selleys), this is what I use myself as it dries quickly to a hard non-crumbly surface. Obtainable at hardware stores. Mix according to instructions, not too much at a time so that it can be spread while creamy.

Clean off all non-patterned areas and level off neatly. If the design is very raised and will need a lot of filling, support the copper on crumpled newspaper or something similar otherwise the weight will cause it to bend.

Plaster of Paris Cheap to buy and usable, generally issued to schools by the Department of Education. The addition of P.V.A. to the water before mixing the Plaster of Paris will help correct the tendency to crack and crumble which can be a problem when you are trying to spread the contact cement. Again, do not mix too much at a time, once it starts to set it will not spread into small areas and cannot be smoothed off. Handle with care when it dries or it will fall out.

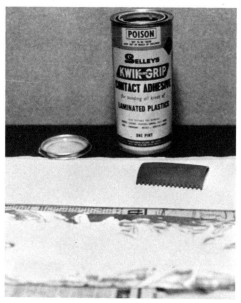

Backing Stiff cardboard, pasteboard or 5 mm Marine Ply can be used, depending on the size and position of the job. For small things such as copper shim tiles, cardboard is suitable, but for articles such as plaques up to about 60 x 90 cm, pasteboard is best. For bigger things like panels for walls, doors or garages use 5 mm Marine Ply, the rigidity is necessary for handling a big piece of work and the waterproof material is essential for outside positions.

The idea of backing is firstly to hold the filling in place, secondly to allow the edges to be neatly turned over making a nice finish and thirdly so that you are able to handle the work until it can be suitably· mounted on a backing board, wall, door or whatever. However, if you are making something like a coffee table top that has wrap round edges, it is simpler to dispense with the backing and apply the contact adhesive to the table top and the back of the copper and then put the **table onto the copper** not vice versa. The filling will not then be disturbed. Make sure that a good seal has been achieved before turning over to finish pressing together.

Measure and cut backing to allow for the copper to turn over all round the edge. Spread contact adhesive thinly on both surfaces, the copper and the backing. When touch dry, fit the backing over the copper so that there is an even amount all round for turning. For really big jobs try Epoxy Contact Cement.

Press the surfaces together as much as possible by slipping one hand under the copper, then turn over the edges, place right side up on a flat surface and smooth all over with your fingers to get rid of any bubbles. Some wrinkles may result but these can be disguised by texturing the background, or left, it does not always detract from the design.

On a really big piece of work this method is too slow. I lie the panel or whatever on a good flat surface, remove my shoes and slide my stockinged feet all over the surface — don't just do the background. It must adhere all over and if properly filled no harm will come to the design if you stand on it.

Note: When doing a really big piece, it is better to smooth out first and turn over the edges last as a certain amount of stretch is possible as you slide round on the surface, and a really neat edge is necessary for appearance sake.

TEXTURING BACKGROUND OF SHIM

While various gadgets for tooling are on the market you can use all kinds of odds and ends and achieve the same result. The round end of your ball pein hammer is good. A round headed nail or screw and various sizes of round headed bolts etc. can be successfully used with a hammer to form a texture. A fine texture can be achieved by hand with the point of your skewer, either as dots or as a design of areas of broken lines which look attractive with some designs.

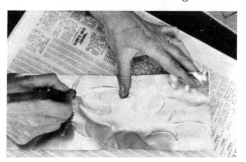

Note: If any areas of heat colouring are to be removed from the background do it before texturing.

Virtually anything that can be repeatedly pressed into the surface either by hand or with a hammer will form a texture. Experiment with any bits and pieces you have around using a scrap piece of shim glued onto a backing. A small length of metal tube will make an interesting pattern as you get a depressed circle with a slightly raised centre — these can be separate or overlapped.

Suit your background treatment to the design — a heavily textured background does not suit a delicate design — in such a case it is often better to leave the background quite plain. Close texturing around a design graduating out to very little at the edges can also look attractive. A design completely made of different kinds of texture in a geometrical type pattern will also work for such things as a panel, a lamp base, a picture, mirror frame, or a modern cube table.

Polishing and finishing

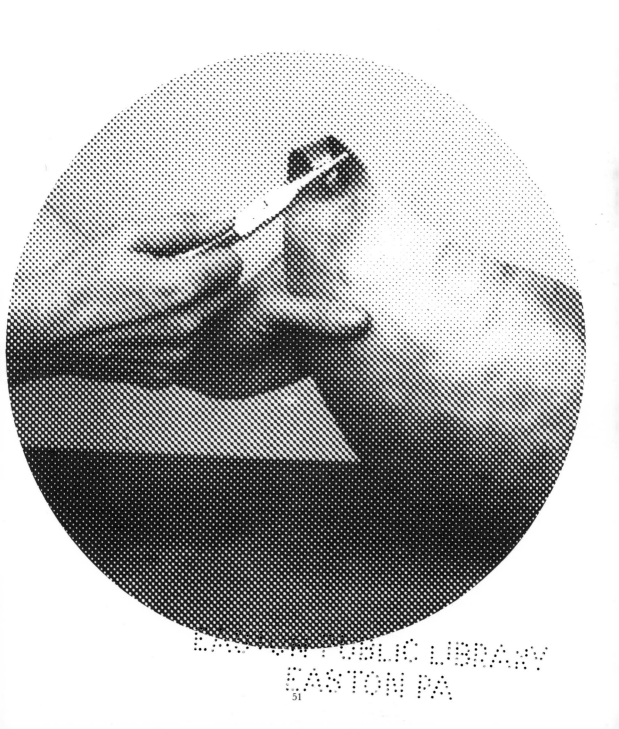

Whether working on a big or small job, shim, sheet copper or wire, anything from an ear-ring to a huge mural, the same amount of care with the polishing and finishing is necessary if you are going to be satisfied with the end result.

COPPER SHIM

By this stage your design has been worked, the colouring process of your choice applied before or after filling and backing, the texturing done if required and you are ready for the final steps.

On an article with no extra colouring at all Brasso can be used lavishly and a great deal of energy expended in achieving a really high polish. However where you want areas of heat colouring or oxidizing to remain, exercise a little caution as it is very easy to go too far and lose the effect you planned. Highlights can be raised by using Brasso on a cloth over your finger or dobbie pad or steel wool followed by vigorous but light polishing with a cloth which has previously been used for Brasso or one only slightly dampened with the metal polish, or by polishing lightly across the design with a Brasso cloth. The constant passage of a soft cloth will highlight the raised parts of the design and though slower, is safer in the long run.

You may wish to polish the design back to the original copper and leave the coloured background, in which case use a little more Brasso on the cloth but be careful not to touch the background which can be buffed up later with a soft cloth. Alternatively, if you want to leave the design coloured, polish off the background using a cloth over your finger but be careful, especially round the edges of the pattern. Finish by polishing all over with a clean soft cloth.

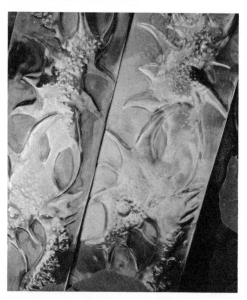

When this stage is finished to your satisfaction, wipe over with thinners to remove any residue. Apply metal lacquer, half and half with 804 thinners, using a soft brush. Allow to dry and apply a second coat. Alternatively spray with copper lacquer, but even a clear wood finish will do if nothing else is available. This will seal the surface from air to prevent tarnishing. **Note:** It is better not to lacquer on a wet or very humid day.

A belt, bracelet, and necklace all coiled in copper wire. Very simple to do and with the minimum of equipment, this jewellery is surprisingly comfortable to wear (See page 62 for instructions).

WAX
A light coating of furniture wax will preserve the colour if applied to the metal while warm (about 32°C) and polished with a soft cloth when thoroughly dry but this is not as satisfactory as some form of lacquer.

JEWELLERY
A little jeweller's buff is invaluable for polishing sheet copper jewellery, but hand polishing achieves the same effect in the end. Waterproof auto-paper, used dry, wet or with a little oil is good for removing scratches and marks. Start with 400 then 500 and 600 for a really smooth finish. Do the final polishing with Brasso and a lot of elbow grease. For articles such as copper pendants with brass overlaid patterns, polish the parts separately before aralditing together. Also polish copper before adding stones if these are to be used. Polish etched bracelets or rings before shaping and give a final finish afterwards. Coiled wire jewellery can be polished with Brasso, highlighted with steel wool and lightly finished with Brasso if oxidized before lacquering.

Hand-made chains are best shined by dipping in copper cleaner, rinsing thoroughly and hanging up to dry before lacquering. If made while the copper is still protected by its coating, it is often not necessary to polish, just dip in thinners and then in metal lacquer (half and half with thinners) and hang on a thin wire to dry. The easiest way is to put a hook of thin wire through a link before dipping and then use it as a hanger. Touch any drips that form with another piece of wire to remove. A better lacquer finish on any copper jewellery is obtained by dipping in the half and half metal lacquer and thinners, rather than spraying. They can all be coated in one operation and this avoids a time lapse when the copper could begin to tarnish. If you can, thread on a wire or in the case of something like a ring or bracelet a loose loop will work just as well, submerge, allow to drip over the container then hang up to dry, removing excess with a wire as for chains.

BEATEN BOWLS
Thoroughly clean, when finished, with copper cleaner and dobbie pad followed by a good rinsing and dry. If you have an electric buff use a cotton buffer and rouge or tripoli. Finish with Brasso and a soft cloth to remove any resultant black marks. Failing that you can take them to a metal workshop and have them professionally polished, or just depend on Brasso and hard work. Beating on a stake with a highly polished planishing

This bracelet, necklace and ring are all worked by coiling copper wire between nails pinned to a board. (See page 69 for instructions.)

hammer will also give a bright finish. Begin at the centre and work in circles towards the edge. Finish with Brasso, or a buff, followed by Brasso.

Whichever method is used give a final rub with thinners before applying several coats of metal lacquer.

ETCHED BOWLS, PLATES

The pattern will show up well if oxidized before polishing by any of the above methods except planishing. However, even polishing will leave a darkened effect on the etched metal. Finish in the same manner. For something like a coffee table top which involves a great deal of work, the baked-on finish is an added protection against wear and tear. A table top 90 x 45 cm cost me approximately $2 which is, to my mind, a good investment.

Joining techniques

Contact Cement

For copper shim, as already dealt with in that section, contact cement is the answer. It will also work when attaching perspex shapes to a copper article. If a large heavy piece is to be joined it is advisable to also add a small screw from the back of the mount into the back of the perspex. As perspex can be drilled this is no problem, and it saves the embarrassment of having a fine piece of work suddenly fall apart, but be discriminate and use only the necessary size of screw to do the job without looking clumsy. Alternatively, drill through the mount and a small distance into the perspex then insert and glue a short length of copper rod.

Epoxy Resin

An epoxy resin comes in two separate tubes, one of resin and one of hardener. These components mixed together in equal parts give an adhesive of great strength. If you are only working on small articles, such as attaching findings to jewellery, a small pack will last a long time (it does not deteriorate) but if you are likely to be using large amounts, for example for a class, the larger pack is much more economical. It can be used for sticking metal to metal, metal to wood, or stones and findings to copper jewellery. Mix on an old saucer or piece of masonite or metal, it is not a good idea to mix on plastic as it reacts with some types. A match or paddle pop stick is handy for both mixing and spreading. Do not be too lavish when spreading as articles should be clamped together until dry and if the adhesive squeezes out it looks unsightly and is very hard to remove. Use a small clamp, cotter pin or spring clothes pin to obtain a tight join while drying, or if flat (a brass or copper inlay or overlay) put under a weight. Under normal drying conditions allow 24 hours, but if a quicker join is required put the article into a pre-heated oven at a temperature of 150° for 30 minutes. Be careful not to overheat or the metal will colour and allow it to cool before taking off the pressure.

Try not to breathe up the fumes while working with epoxy resin and handle carefully to avoid contact with the skin. However, if you inadvertently get some on your fingers mineral turps will remove it.

There are fast-setting epoxy resins, suitable for fastening stones to jewellery, but they are generally less strong.

Solder

There are occasions when soldering cannot be avoided. For strong durable joints e.g. edge joints, hard or silver solder is required. This needs a high temperature to melt. As it is silver in colour, as the name suggests, use with care so that it is not obvious on the copper or it will look amateurish. It can be filed back when cold, to neaten. A less strong join can be obtained with soft solder, which, because it is a combination of lead and tin, has a lower melting point. Tinmans Solder, which is a good one to use, is 50-50 with a melting point of 216°C. There are also various very low melting point solders (Tape Solder) on the market which will melt with the heat of a match on a small job, or with a pin point flame on something bigger, but naturally they aren't very strong. Though principally for pewter it can be handy to solder enamelled pieces.

Whichever method you are using a few basic rules apply.

1. The metal must be clean. Prepare by rubbing well with steel wool or fine wet and dry. Any grease, wax, dirt or oxidizing will prevent the solder from flowing. Even oil from the fingers will cause trouble.

2. A good fit. Whether joining wire to wire, wire to sheet copper, or sheet to sheet, the pieces must actually **make contact** and be **held in contact** while heat is applied. Careful preparation pays dividends, time spent here is better than time wasted in having to start again and do the job properly. In some instances the weight of the metal (for example when attaching a brass overlay piece to a copper pendant with soft solder) will provide a good contact. If not, some other method must be used. For joining an article like a box, iron binding wire is the answer. Always twist a loop into the wire opposite the ends before twisting them together. This can then be used for tightening and gets a much better pressure.

Wire clamps or clips are very useful. Spring type wooden clothes pegs can be used if wet, or you may find that holding the article in a vice works well.

3. Flux, if necessary, must be the correct kind. Some solders have their own flux incorporated, but check when buying. Silphos is a hard solder that requires no flux, otherwise a good paste is easy to use with a silver solder, and can be applied with a small brush. For a soft solder some companies make a liquid flux in a plastic bottle with a fine nipple, or if you prefer, keep a little paint brush for the job.

Tape Solder requires no extra flux. The purpose of the flux is to prevent oxidization of the metal by heat before the solder can flow, so if in doubt, it is better to use it than not to.

Silver Solder

This is generally in wire or rod form. Rub it with steel wool to clean and cut it with Wiss cutters into pieces about 1 mm long onto a piece of paper or into a lid or similar receptacle so you don't lose it! Having applied flux to your clean metal use your brush to pick up the pieces of solder and place about 3 mm apart along the join. Try to use only enough solder to fill the join and hold the metal together. Place the object on a fire-proof surface e.g. asbestos, fire bricks, or metal grill on a tripod, and slowly preheat the surrounding metal, not the solder, until the water dries out of the flux. If the boiling flux dislodges the solder from position push it back, once the flux dries out it will hold in place. Continue heating the metal round the join until it becomes slightly red and the flux will again become liquid. Concentrate heat on the join and the solder will flow towards the heat. Immediately the solder flows remove the flame. When the job has cooled, remove the binding wire or clamping device and clean in pickle or copper cleaner to remove oxide and fire hardened flux from the metal. Wash thoroughly and dry. An easy way to dry jewellery without leaving water marks is to place in a pan of heated sawdust.

Soft Solder
Used primarily to attach jewellery findings to pins and ear-rings, if you prefer it to epoxy resin. However, bear in mind that you are going to oxidize the article which must then be carefully cleaned again. Whether using Tinmans solder or the coil variety, clean with steel wool then hammer out very flat before cutting in small pieces. Clean the surfaces thoroughly, apply flux and small amounts of solder, clamp together if necessary, put on a metal grill and heat from underneath with only enough heat to melt. In the case of the pendant which was not clamped, you will see the overlay settle at the moment of melting. Remove heat immediately and allow to cool before touching. Rinse, then clean in pickle and wash well. Some findings have a little cup into which the soft solder can be melted then positioned and reheated. If stones are to be incorporated in the design, solder first and glue these after recleaning the copper.

Sweat Soldering
This method is employed if applying decorative wire to sheet metal and is done by first tinning the wire (applying a thin layer of solder either hard or soft onto the wire), re-fluxing, clamping into position and reheating until the solder flows into the join. If required for cloisonné enamelling use a silver solder because of the higher melting point. Clean as before prior to using enamel.

Copper jewellery without solder

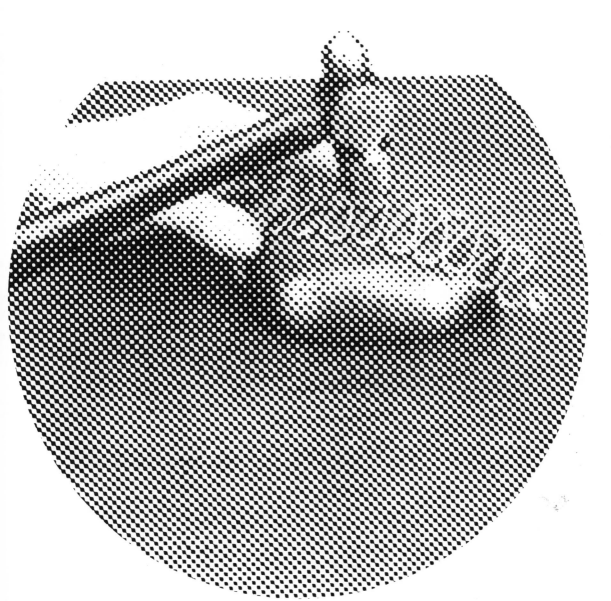

One of the easiest techniques to master in jewellery making is coiling wire into links which can then be assembled into bracelets, necklets and belts. Plain wire, twisted wire, polished or oxidized, there are endless variations on the same theme. Even primary school children can handle it and get a great deal of satisfaction out of making something attractive and useful for themselves or for gifts.

You will need few tools. A wire cutter (your Wiss cutters if you have them); a pair of round jewellery pliers; a pair of half round jewellery pliers (or even an ordinary pair of small pliers will do); plus the usual polishing and finishing Brasso, soft cloth, coppertoner, if you wish to oxidize, metal lacquer and 804 thinners.

Key to Photo
Back: Brasso, Coppertoner, metal lacquer, Chain and ball for end of belt.
Left to Right: Round jewellery pliers, half round jewellery pliers, 25 cm length of wire with circle on each end, coiled each end, bent in middle, shank bent over level with coils, two linked together, 3 coil bracelets.
Foreground: section of coiled belt in twisted wire.
Opposite:
Matching set of etched copper jewellery using masking tape. (See step-by-step instructions on page 78.)
Page 64:
Three etched plates; the plate in the foreground is etched by the use of hard ground; on the left and above two plates using resist paint, the positive has a raised pattern and the negative a depressed one. (See page 81 and 83 for instructions.)

COILED BRACELET IN 16 GAUGE WIRE
(See photograph on page 53.)

Coiled bracelet in 16g. wire implements

1. Cut 14 25 cm lengths of copper wire.
2. With your round jewellery pliers turn a small circle on each end of each piece.
3. Change to the flat faced pliers and holding the small circle, firmly pull the wire around to make a coil, moving the pliers as you proceed. Repeat on the opposite end and coil an equal number of circles until the overall length is 6.5 cm. Do the same on each piece of wire.
4. Bend each piece in half, either with your fingers, or by pulling round a nail, then bend the resulting shank over so that it lies level with the lower edge of the coils.
5. By slipping one shank through the next, link all the pieces together except the last one.
6. Going back to the first link, slip the coils of the last link (the 14th) under the existing ones and pull up so that they lie flat and the hook of the shank makes one end of the fastening.

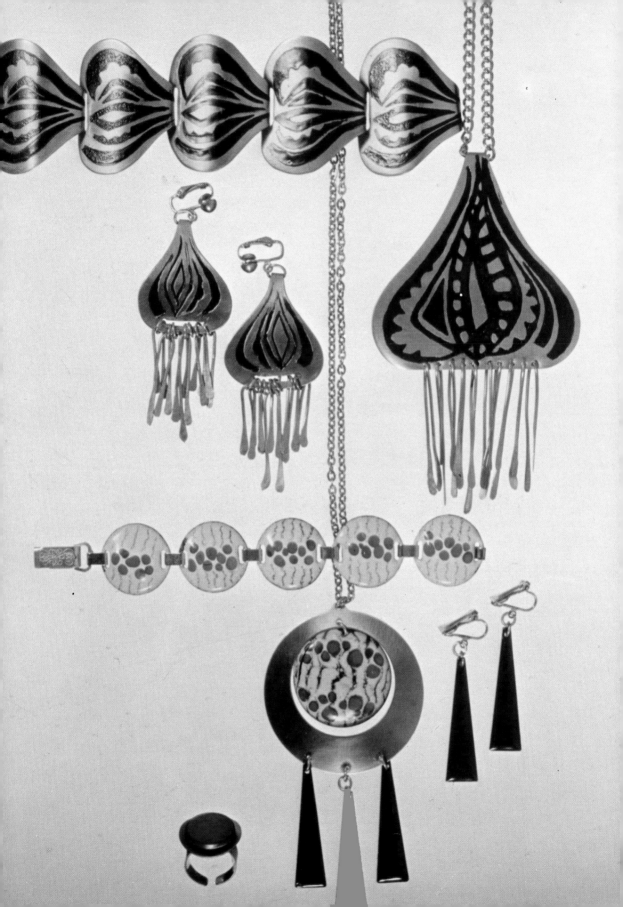

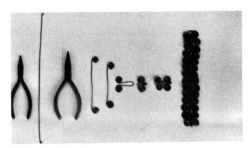

Coiled bracelet step by step

7. With the half round pliers, press the shank at the opposite end flat instead of round, to take the fastening hook more easily.

8. Place the bracelet flat on the table and with your fingers press the coils down so that they lie close together, on either side of the central links.

9. Polish with Brasso, attach to a fine wire, dip in metal lacquer and 804 thinners 50-50, hang up to dry after allowing to drip over the container. (See finishing section).

If Antique finish is desired, mix Coppertoner as directed, dip in hot solution after polishing, hang up to dry, rub up highlights lightly with steel wool, lacquer finish as above.

MATCHING COIL NECKLACE IN COPPER WIRE

Proceed as for the bracelet, but make enough links to fit comfortably around the neck. Add a short chain to one end and a short chain and hook to the other for easy adjustment.

HOW TO TWIST WIRE USING A DRILL

Take a coil of wire and unroll it. Slip the centre through a strong hook or over a strong peg of some kind and holding the two ends together place them into a hand or electric drill (instead of a bit) and screw up very tightly. Step back until there is a moderate tension on the wires to hold them evenly together. Turn the drill until the desired amount of twist is achieved. This will be beautifully even.

Note: Take care if using an electric drill, the maximum amount of twist the wire can take is achieved in a flash and the wire will then snap and could be dangerous for anybody standing in the vicinity as it whips about.

The gauge wire you use depends on what you are going to use it for. For a bracelet 18 gauge is heavy enough, even 20 gauge can look delicate and pretty, 16 gauge is okay for a belt or a wall sculpture, even 14 gauge will twist well with the fingers and look quite impressive except for tight patterns.

COILED BELT IN TWISTED WIRE

For a 5 cm wide belt, twist a quantity of 16 gauge wire (2 coils) and cut 26 pieces 40 cm long (this will make a hipster belt approximately 71 cm long plus the chain fastening

Page 65:
An etched table top, 90 x 45 cm, in 20 gauge copper. The design is a detail from 'The Witches' textile, Hispano Moresque, twelfth century, now in the Archaeological and Artistic Museum, Barcelona. The method used was Asphaltum as a block-out, applied with a very fine brush, and concentrated nitric acid and water as an etching agent.

Opposite:
At the top of the picture, jewellery is etched by the Champlevé method. (See description on page 77.) The ear-rings and bracelet are done by the masking tape method, but the pendant is resist paint etched. The red, black and white jewellery is enamelled and can be fired by either a gas torch or a kiln. (See instructions on page 92.)

which can be adjusted). Proceed as for the bracelet but because of the heavier wire make the coils a little looser, and about 15 cm overall length when coiled at each end.

Actual size of each link

When bending in the centre hold with flat faced pliers so that the end of the link is square. This makes an easier fitting join. Attach the last coil to the first to form a hook.

To Make the Chain
Wrap the twisted wire tightly round a 13 mm dowel or rod of some kind, twice for each link you require in the chain. Slip off and cut through every second circle with the Wiss cutters and fit together. Any sharp cut ends should be filed smooth.

Ornament for end of Chain
Using the twisted wire and with the round jewellery pliers make a small circle in the end. With the flat faced pliers, coil the wire as for the links but close together until five or six circles have been made. Then working on top of these, coil back towards the centre, doing the smallest one with the round jewellery pliers. Cut off leaving a 2 cm length of wire. Form a loop with this, slipping the cut end down the centre of the middle circle for a neat finish.

With fingers or pliers, separate the coils and stretch them out to form a ball shape. Attach to the chain through the loop and pass the link at the opposite end of the chain through the end of the belt and you have an adjustable fastening.

MAKING YOUR OWN CHAINS
While it is quick and convenient to use bought chains there are many attractive ways to make your own. Copper wire of various gauges can be used, as well as such things as copper boat nails, small copper washers, various shapes of sheet copper, small copper blanks or lengths of rectangular copper section, used alone with jump rings or in various combinations.

The easiest method is to wrap copper wire over a round, square or oblong rod or piece of metal then cut with a fine hacksaw and join the links together using two pairs of jewellery pliers. Separate the rings sideways, rather than forcing them open as this will spoil their shape and make it harder to put them back into a close join.

A quick method is to cut a number of equal lengths of copper wire, then join them by forming an S with your round jewellery pliers and closing them tightly together. The longer the length of the shank between the ends, the quicker the chain will be made. Lengths with a circle turned on each end can be put together in twos or threes with a single jump ring or copper wire ring between. There are endless varieties. Sixteen gauge copper cut in lengths up to 7 cm can be hammered flat, curled at each end and joined with rings.

To make a chain with boat nails, buy a few 3 cm nails (they are quite expensive), cut off the heads then hammer them flat on each end. Shape nicely with a file and drill a hole in each end. Add a texture to the square part of the nail with the round end of your ball pein hammer. Clean with steel wool, polish, join together with rings, and dip in metal lacquer. Hang to dry. A hook can be easily made with a piece of copper wire if the chain is too short to go over your head.

Another quite effective method is to wind lengths of wire around a rod. Do not cut them into rings, instead leave in tubular lengths just twisting a loop on each end to join them together.

Fine copper wire, 28g. or 30g., can be worked on a daisy wheel or old fashioned cotton reel and nails (with the heads cut off) like those children use for French knitting to make a tubular 'rope' which has many uses. With a motif attached to each end it can be hung round the neck and casually looped in front.

WIRE BRACELET
(See photograph on page 54.)
Requirements
14 gauge wire; Wiss cutters; piece of pineboard or similar; 2.5 cm panel pins; jeweller's dolly; round jewellery pliers; hammer.

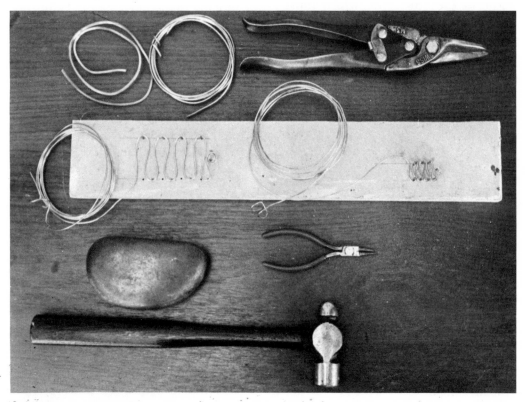

Wire bracelet implements in 14g. wire

On the pineboard draw two parallel lines 5 cm apart and mark out in 2 cm, offset, i.e. the lower row coming not opposite, but in between, for a distance of 15 cm or the required length of the bracelet, allowing for it to spread a little. Hammer the panel pins well into the board and snip off the heads.

Take the pliers and make a coil of three or four rounds, this will form one end of the clip. Slip a panel pin through the centre and hammer into the board half way between the two lines and you are ready to start the pattern. Holding the wire taut twist it up and down round the panel pins. **(Step 1)** Remove from the board and cut the wire allowing enough to form a coil at the other end, which must come on the opposite loop from the first one, i.e. if the fastener on the first loop faces upwards, then at the last loop it must face downwards to ensure a close join.

Lay the bracelet over the dolly and lightly hammer on the loops to flatten and work-harden as this gives spring and resilience. **(Step 2)** If the loops part, work along with your fingers pressing them back close together again, at the same time shaping into a circle. This may sound complicated, but with the wire in your hands you will find it simple. **(Step 3)** With the pliers, ease the coils up from the loops

so that they will slip one through the other and make a neat fastening.

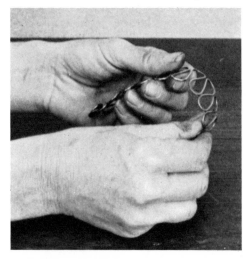

Polish with Brasso and lacquer by dipping in metal lacquer as before and hang up to dry.

On the right hand end of the board in the photograph for step 1 you will see a ring made by the same method, with the lines 2 cm apart and spaces 6 mm. A hair ornament for a pony tail, or chignon is also easily made by this method. Sketch out the shape on the board and work as before, the coil at each end takes the pin, and an extra little twist in the pattern adds interest. The pin, which is made from a 12 cm length of the wire has a circle at one end. The shank is hammered flat, and the opposite end is filed to a blunt point. It can be left separate, or attached through the ring to the ornament with a piece of fine chain long enough for it to be slipped in and out.

The same technique done in a finer gauge wire can be used for a choker on which to hang another shape in different gauge wire, a stone in a setting, a piece of enamel, or built up in rows from the initial one, to form a more intricate necklace. Once you get the feel of the design you will find it quite easy to do it with your fingers without the nails as a guide.

ZODIAC PENDANT: ARIES
(See photograph on page 37.)
Cut a shape in 20 gauge sheet copper, allowing enough at the top to bend over and form a holder for the chain. With a ball pein hammer, texture the surface. File and smooth the edges, clean thoroughly and polish, oxidize with sulphurate potash and when dry buff up with a soft cloth.
cloth.

Cut two 12 cm lengths of square wire, and file the ends into a nice smooth shape. The ends which will form the nose should also be bevelled towards the lower edge of the pendant to look more natural. With the pliers bend the first piece into a nice curve and, using it as a pattern, bend the second to match but the opposite way. Glue to the backing piece after polishing well, and clamp until dry.

PENDANT WITH ABSTRACT SETTING FOR 2 STONES
Cut a nice shape in 20 gauge (or 18g.) copper sheet, file and smooth the edges with steel wool, drill a hole for the chain, clean and polish both sides.

With the pliers, bend a piece of 12 gauge copper wire into a shape that will fit neatly around the stones (available real or synthetic at craft shops). To add form to the design flatten in places on the jewellery dolly with your ball pein hammer. Smooth with steel wool, and polish. Assemble with epoxy resin and finish with metal lacquer as described.

PENDANT WITH SWINGING SHAPE
Requirements
6 mm rectangular copper section, 18g. sold in 61 cm lengths; (This pendant takes 20 cm so one length will make 3 with various free swinging shapes, or the balance will be handy for such things as rings. As the edges have a rounded finish it is very quick to use.) Short length of $\frac{1}{2}$ round 12g. copper wire (or whatever you fancy to dangle in the centre); 2 jump rings; chain.

Cut a 2 cm piece from the 20 cm length and neatly finish the four ends with a file rounding off the corners. Clean all over with steel wool then polish. Drill a small hole at each end of the small piece — one is to attach the jump ring for the chain, the other holds a jump ring to suspend the centre motif. On the long piece, with round jewellery pliers, bend a small half circle at each end, then press over something round, the Brasso tin will do, but something slightly smaller would be better, to form a nice circle. Glue the small piece between the two ends with resin pressing together firmly with a spring clip. Make sure that they all line up neatly, and that the position allows both holes to be accessible.

With the pliers twist the piece of wire into a nice shape, small enough to swing freely inside the circle and with a ring or loop at the top to go through the jump ring. When the resin has dried, assemble, polish, dip in metal lacquer and thinners and hang up to dry.

COPPER PENDANT WITH BRASS OVERLAY
Requirements

Wiss cutters; file, also needle files; steel wool; piece of 20 gauge copper approximately 4 x 9 cm; Nibblers; piece of scrap brass, 20 gauge; hand drill and bits; epoxy resin; Brasso, metal lacquer if desired.

Cut round corners on one end of your piece of copper. With a file smooth the edges and slightly round the other two corners. Clean both sides and the edges with steel wool. Measure, punch and drill a small hole for attaching a chain and smooth off any burr. Polish with Brasso, also clean and polish the piece of brass.

With the nibblers, bite a pattern round the brass until it appeals to you.

(Step 1) With a needle file smooth off any sharp corners and edges. **(Step 2)**

If you decide to add some holes mark with a centre punch or nail, place between two pieces of scrap three-ply to protect the metal from damage and fasten firmly in a vice to drill. **(Step 3)** Never have somebody hold brass for you with their fingers. When the bit 'bites' into the metal it will spin dangerously and can cause a nasty injury. If neatening is necessary, do it with the round needle file.

A final polish of both pieces and you are ready for the resin. Spread thinly and clamp firmly or cover with a piece of paper and a flat weight until set.

Lacquer finish can be added if desired. However on a piece such as this I prefer to leave it as it is and polish it with a little Brasso and a soft cloth when I have occasion to wear it. Constant polishing, which only takes a minute, enriches the colour, the Brasso leaves a greenish patina round the join which accentuates the pattern and it seems to become more attractive as time goes by. However, it is purely a personal choice. On most articles of jewellery it would be difficult to be constantly polishing and the lacquer finish is a must.

ETCHED PENDANT

See instructions for etching on page 74, and use resin to set the stone into the centre of the etched design.

Etching

Etching is an ancient craft which enables an image to be cut into a metal surface whether for decorative purposes or to produce a multiple number of prints from one drawing on a metal plate. It is done by the use of acid and a resist material and several different methods can be employed on copper according to the desired end result.

Very attractive etched jewellery, rings, bracelets, pendants, belts, etc. can be produced easily using masking tape to protect the copper from the nitric acid. This method is most suitable for a classroom as it eliminates waiting for the resist paint to dry. It is not messy and is easier to produce a pattern with a neat straight edge. It is best for small articles but can be used on larger pieces provided they are flat and a good seal is made on the joins of the masking tape. After the copper has been prepared and thoroughly cleaned it is completely sealed in masking tape, the design applied and the parts required to be 'bitten' down by the acid are cut out with a razor blade (Gem) or some kind of small sharp cutting tool and removed.

Note: Never, in any type of etching, have a design that goes right to the edge as this will lead to problems.

The piece is then immersed in a bath of 50-50 concentrated nitric acid and water. **Remember** always add the acid to the water, never vice versa. After a few minutes, when the acid has eaten sufficiently into the copper (as explained in instructions for etched bracelet on page 78) it is removed, rinsed, stripped of the masking tape, washed, polished and finished.

The second method is to use resist paint of a bituminous nature.

It is suitable for most articles — jewellery, bowls, plates, tiles, table tops and pictures, in fact the size is only restricted by the receptacle for holding the acid. If you are very ambitious even this can be overcome. When faced with the problem of etching a 90 x 45 cm table top (see picture on page 65) I solved it by using four pieces of 4 x 4 timber, arranged in the right dimensions, plus a sheet of heavy builder's plastic with plenty of overlap which I depressed into the centre of the improvised frame and weighted well round the outside edges so it could not possibly slip and spill the acid. As a large quantity of acid was required, enough to cover by about 6 mm all over on a flat surface, I did it in my backyard on a windy day to disperse the fumes. If tackling a job of this size remember that the surface on which you arrange your plastic must be level as an uneven depth of acid will result in an uneven depth of etch.

After cleaning and preparing your copper, first paint the back of the article and allow it to dry for 24 hours. Prepare your design, put it on with carbon paper and paint carefully with a fine sable hair brush on the parts you want to reproduce. Whether you remove the background and leave the design, or remove the design and leave the background is entirely a matter of taste. In fact I like to make plates in

An enamelled necklace, made in five separate pieces and chained together. (See page 98 for instructions.)

pairs, positive and negative. If you have an attractive design it is very decorative to have a pair, and makes a good conversation piece. However, if removing the background, always remember to leave a border to protect the edge of the article. Also be very careful that the edge is completely masked with paint. Allow to dry for another 24 hours if possible. If any parts show up brownish instead of black, touch with more paint as these could break up in the acid and leave a blemish on the surface where you least want it. Any fine details, e.g. veins in leaves, can be scratched through the surface of the paint with a needle or point of a pair of compasses after the paint has dried.

Put the article carefully into the acid bath as before until the etch is sufficiently deep. Rinse well, remove the resist paint with mineral turpentine and polish with Brasso. The etched surface is slightly rough and will darken with the Brasso, this makes the pattern more obvious. However, if you so desire you can colour with Coppertoner (see oxidizing and colouring section on page 43), polish and lacquer.

Either of the above methods can be used to etch articles for enamelling later using the Champlevé or Basse-taille methods. Champlevé is a process of enamelling where a design is etched into the metal and enamel applied into these depressions and fired. (See jewellery on page 66.) When all the necessary colours have been added the surface is rubbed down with a fine file, stone of Ayr or buff, so that the enamel is level with the metal surround, then refired to restore the gloss to the enamel. Polish and lacquer finish the job.

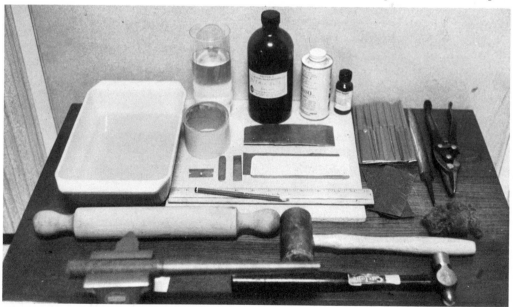

Materials for etched bracelet and ring.

Opposite:
Two enamelled boxes done in a kiln. (See page 95 for instructions.)

Basse-taille, on the other hand is completely covered with transparent enamel, which, being of greater thickness in the etched design, gives a variation in depth of colour which can be very attractive. The copper shines up through the transparency.

HOW TO MAKE AN ETCHED BRACELET AND RING
(See photograph on page 63)
Requirements
22 gauge copper for bracelet — 15 x 5 cm; 20 gauge copper for ring — 6 x 1.3 cm; Wiss cutters; ruler; 15 cm file; steel wool; copper cleaner or vinegar and salt and dobbie pad for cleaning copper; Biro; suitable design; carbon paper; masking tape; gem razor blade; concentrated nitric acid — mix in a pyrex dish or thick plastic container with 50 per cent water 50 per cent acid.
(Caution: always add the acid gradually to the water, stirring all the time. Never add water to acid. Use in well ventilated area with a fan.) Brasso and soft cloth: oxidation preparation; rolling pin or 5 cm diameter dowel for shaping bracelet; ring mandrell for shaping ring; small vice; leather mallet; metal lacquer and 804 thinners.

Step 1. Cut copper to size and flatten with the leather mallet on a firm surface e.g. a piece of pineboard.

Step 2. Holding firmly in the hand, file the edges.

Step 3. Round the corners, then rub right round the edge with steel wool. Clean thoroughly all over with copper cleaner, or vinegar and salt, and dobbie pad, rinse and dry, do not put your fingers on the surface, hold carefully by edges.

Step 4. Completely cover with masking tape, pressing on firmly and sealing well so that no acid can penetrate.

Step 5. Put the design on masking tape with carbon and Biro — be sure there is a plain border so that the acid cannot spoil the edge.

Step 6. Cut around the design with a gem razor blade and remove the background areas which will then be exposed to the acid.

Step 7. Using wooden or copper tongs, carefully place the copper in the prepared acid. When the bubbles begin to rise, brush with a feather held

above the copper. Be sure that the container is level or the etch will not be even.

Step 8. After about 5-10 minutes, remove the copper with tongs, rinse well under running water. Test with a fingernail to check that the etch is deep enough. If not, return to the acid and repeat the procedure. In freshly mixed acid 5 minutes should be enough, on re-using, 10 minutes or longer may be necessary.

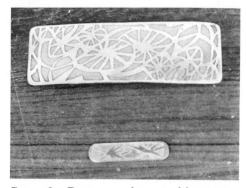

Step 9. Remove the masking tape after thorough rinsing, then wash again. If any sticky residue is left from the tape, remove with turpentine. Polish with Brasso and a soft cloth.

Step 10. Colour with preparation if
desired, polish lightly when dry,
secure a rolling pin or 5 cm dowel in a
vice for the bracelet and beat into
shape with the leather mallet. Do the
same for the ring on a ring mandrell.
Step 11. Give a final polish if
necessary, wipe with thinners, hang on
a loop of fine wire, dip in lacquer
(50-50 with 804 thinners), hold above
the container to drip, then hang up to
dry.

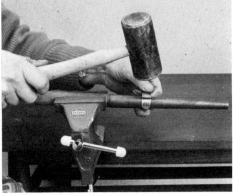

INSTRUCTIONS FOR TWO ETCHED PLATES USING RESIST PAINT

(See photograph on page 64)
Requirements

Two 18 cm turned shallow plates; Asphaltum or Plymel paint; Fine Sable Brush for design; larger brush for back; Turpentine; Design; carbon paper; Biro; Scotch tape; Acid bath as for etched bracelet; Brasso; soft cloth; lacquer.

Step 1. Clean and prepare the plates as in the previous instructions. Paint the backs with resist paint and allow to dry 24 hours.

Step 2. Using Scotch tape, secure the carbon and design to the first plate and outline firmly with a Biro. As I wished to remove the design and leave the background I painted the **background** with resist paint.

Note: The design must not go right to the edge. Always have a border, even if it is very narrow.

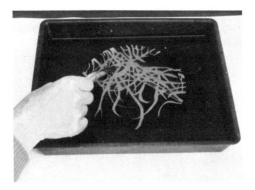

Step 3. Place in an acid bath and agitate acid with a feather to remove bubbles as they form. Remove with wooden tongs after five minutes, rinse and test depth.

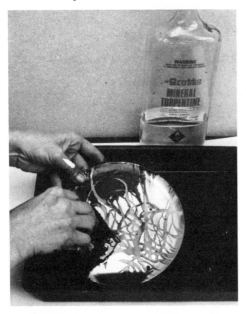

Step 4. Remove resist paint with turpentine.

Polish with Brasso and a soft cloth. Apply metal lacquer and thinners 50-50, two coats, back and front. Repeat this process reversing the design treatment, that is using the same design, again paint the design and leave the background to etch.

Plique-à-jour is also a combination of etching and enamelling, but definitely not for the beginner. It is double etching, which means that the identical design is applied to both back and front and allowed to slow etch until it goes right through the metal (a quicker method of course would be to pierce the metal with a drill and hacksaw or needle file). The hole is then filled with damp transparent enamel and if the holes are small enough it will stay in place by capillary attraction until fired, or, if larger are fired over a sheet of mica which is then removed. The light shines through the enamelled parts like tiny jewels or pieces of a stained glass window.

While on the subject of double etching, it works beautifully on thin copper — 28 gauge to make delicate ear-rings (these can be done with masking tape) or such things as butterfly wings using the resist paint. On butterfly wings, slightly offset the design so that an exact etch is not achieved and where there is a half etched edge it looks like the 'velvet' on real wings when polished.

Soft ground and hard ground are two methods of etching used for printing plates but can also be used on decorative plates and bowls. This means meticulous preparation if the copper plate is to be used for printing because not a single blemish must remain to mar the surface. Whether for printing or pleasure, the surface should be cleaned with vinegar and salt, rinsed well and then diligently rubbed with wet and dry sand paper, starting with 400, then 500 and 600, finally cleaning with Brasso, then whiting and ammonia, rinsing well and drying.

The article is then heated over a low heat. The soft or hard ground, which you can buy from an art supplier in a 'knob' and which is a combination of beeswax and asphalt is then pressed against the warm metal so that it adheres in spots. A dauber (this can be made by tightly rolling a nylon stocking into a mushroom shape) is then used to spread the 'ground' in an even film over the surface. In the case of hard ground if a **really** hard surface is required for fine lines, it is then smoked with a taper or candle. The back is then coated with resist paint (asphaltum or plymel) allowed to dry and the design applied. With soft ground the pressure of a pencil or Biro through the design on paper will transfer it into the surface. With hard ground a sharp tool is used to scratch through the wax, then it is placed in the nitric acid solution (or Dutch Mondant for a fine slow etch), rinsed, cleaned with turps, then whiting and ammonia rinsed, dried, and used for printing, or polished, lacquered and admired.

STEP-BY-STEP INSTRUCTIONS FOR A DECORATIVE PLATE USING HARD GROUND.

(See photograph on page 64)

Requirements

Turned Plate; Hard ground; Dauber Heat (Torch or Hot Plate); Asphaltum; candle; sharp instrument; turpentine; acid bath; Brasso; Lacquer.

Step 1. Clean and prepare the plate according to the instructions in the etching section (page 78)

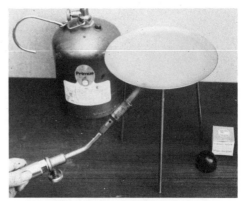

Step 2. Heat gently with a gas torch (or on a hot plate). **Do not overheat.**

Step 3. With the hard ground 'knob', press spots onto the warm metal.

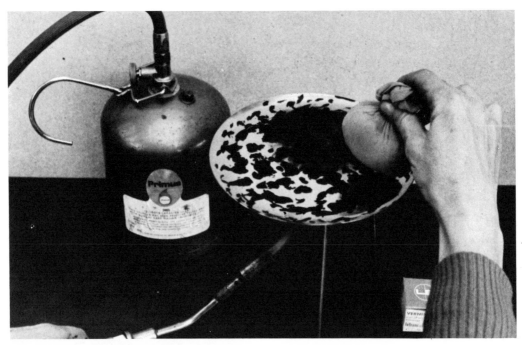

Step 4 (above) Using the dauber spread onto an even film.

Step 5. Hold the plate firmly in the left hand and with the right smoke the surface with a candle or taper flame. Keep rotating the flame until the sooty look disappears and a shining black surface results. Do not hold the flame too close.

Step 6. Paint the back of the plate with asphaltum and allow to dry for 24 hours (when painting be sure to seal the edge).

Step 7. Place your paper design on the hard ground with Scotch tape. Trace around with a Biro and firm pressure so that the impression will show on the surface.

Step 8. With a darning needle or etching tool scratch through the surface, but be careful not to dig into the copper.

Step 9. Place in 50-50 concentrated nitric acid and water as described for etched bracelet (page 78).

Step 10. As the lines are fine and therefore take longer to etch, check after 10 minutes to see if the etch is deep enough. When etched to your satisfaction, rinse well under running water, remove hard ground and resist paint with turpentine. Polish and lacquer.

Enamelling techniques

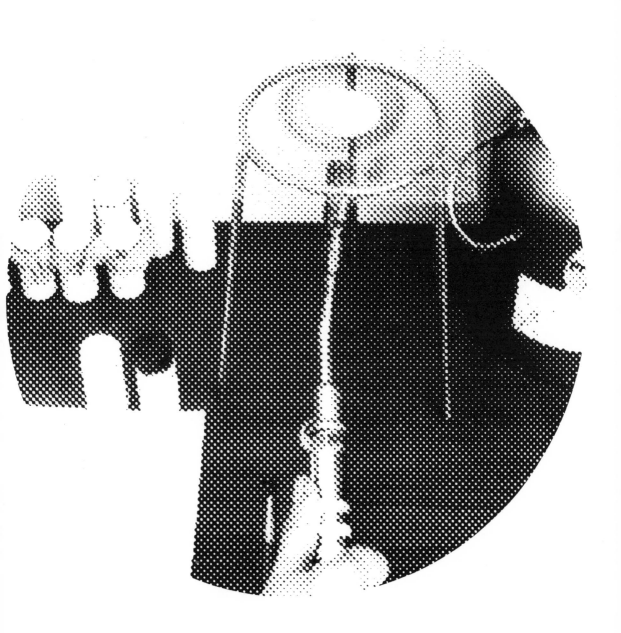

Enamelling is a very ancient craft which never seems to lose its popularity. Probably because not many tools are necessary, the techniques are basically simple and the results can be seen almost immediately. Apart from this the colours are many, varied and can be glowingly beautiful. Of course, as in most crafts, there are pitfalls for the unwary or impatient, but even young children can produce some quite surprisingly attractive articles.

Enamel is basically a combination of flux (clear glass) and metal oxides (for colour) finely ground together. When applied to metal and fired for a short time, it fuses onto the surface giving a bright glassy finish. The heat source can be either a gas torch for small pieces or an enamelling kiln, the size of your piece is restricted only by the internal dimensions of the kiln. It is simpler to get a good result with a kiln where the heat is even and can be regulated by a pyrometer, but if you have only a gas tank, don't be deterred! Invest in a tripod and a good strong stainless steel gauge and go to it. Remember that in jewellery, large pieces can be built up from small units so use your imagination and the available facilities to the limit.

Copper is an excellent metal for enamelling, it has a higher melting point than the enamel, which of course is essential, but as a general rule, use no lighter than 20 gauge or you will be disappointed. The metal will distort if it is too thin and the enamel will shatter.

Nineteen gauge, from which the ready cut blanks and spun bowls are made, or 18 gauge, will give the best results. I used 22 gauge for the Champlevé bracelet and ear-rings because 20 gauge would have been too heavy to wear, but this was a little different as the enamel is in small patterns and actually quite thin. In the usual course of events the thickness of the finished enamel should equal the thickness of the copper. Thinly applied enamel powder tends to go patchy and burn back on the edges when fired.

ENAMELS

Three different kinds of enamels can be used, transparent, opaque and opalescent, the first two are the most popular with the average enameller. Opalescent colours are harder to use and are for more experienced craftsmen and special designs. While dedicated craftsmen buy the frit (glass) and grind it themselves with a hard porcelain mortar and pestle (available at a chemists' supplier), for the average hobbyist it is simpler to buy the prepared powder enamel available in 1oz or 4oz bottles at craft and hobby shops. Suppliers generally have sample sheets showing the colour straight over copper, over colourless flux and in the case of transparents, over white opaque, so that you have a good idea of the shades before you buy them. Schauer brand enamels are the best known and are the type supplied to schools. The colours are all numbered, labelled Transparent or Opaque as the case may be and generally show the approximate firing temperature. This saves guess work and helps with re-ordering.

Opaque Enamel

This means that you cannot see the copper through it. The depth of colour can be enhanced by firing a layer of transparent enamel over a layer of opaque. When using more than one colour in a design always fire each one separately. This, as well as being easier to manage, saves wastage. Always work on a large sheet of clean paper with a small piece under your work. A piece already creased in half is best and the kind of toilet tissue that comes in separate squares with a centre fold is excellent. This ensures easy return of excess powder to its glass tube. This should be done immediately after use to guard against mixing up your colours. Keep any that become inadvertently mixed in a separate container and used for counter enamelling as colours will not mix together, like paint, to make a third colour. Each grain remains separate to give a tweedy effect rather muddy in appearance. However, it is excellent for counter enamelling (enamelling the backs of large pieces to prevent the enamel from cracking because it stabilizes the metal by equalizing the tension in the expansion and contraction caused by heating).

Opaque enamels do not need washing so you can use them straight out of the glass container. However, when enamelling, always use the greatest precautions to keep everything clean, free from dust and flying pieces of fire scale which pop off articles when removed from the kiln. These can get into uncovered enamels or onto a piece you have prepared for firing and ruin the final result. For the same reason always clean the backs and edges of pieces with steel wool, or copper cleaner and dobbie pad between firings to remove the fire scale. Do this away from your enamelling bench as soon as the work is cool and wipe up the loose pieces which have fallen off by themselves.

It is important, in order not to waste your enamel powder, to return the excess to the container immediately after use. If loose fire scale is allowed to remain on the back of the piece, when applying the next colour it will become mixed with the powder and ruin it, even for counter enamelling.

Transparent Enamel

This allows the metal to shine through the colour (unless, of course, you use an undercoat of opaque). While opaque enamel can be used straight from the tube, transparent should always be washed in order to achieve clear beautiful colours, impurities give a milky appearance.

Place the transparent enamel powder in a glass or glass jar, and add plenty of water. Stir well. The water will become cloudy with a greyish powder. Allow enamel to settle a little, then pour off the liquid. Repeat 3 or 4 times until the water appears to be clear. If possible, distilled water should be used for the final wash to avoid any impurities. When you have drained off as much water as possible spread the wet enamel powder on a flat dish and leave to dry in a warm place. If the washing water is poured into a container and left to settle you will be able to salvage some powder to add to your counter enamelling jar — but dry it first!

Colourless Flux

This makes a good base coat, especially under transparents, which are not as easy to use as opaques, but are inclined to pull back from the edges or to separate leaving spaces which burn and are difficult to clean for re-firing. Copper cleaner will do the job but if used for any length of time it takes the colour out of the enamel.

White or grey opaque also makes a good base coat under transparent but if you wish to preserve the effect of the copper shining through then colourless flux is the answer. It can also be used as a base coat under opaques if you wish, but unless you are very careful it comes up as clear speckles through successive coats.

CLEANING

Always clean your copper thoroughly before enamelling to remove the protective coating and any dirt or grease that has accumulated through handling or just lying around. For jewellery pieces, clean thoroughly with vinegar and salt and steel wool as explained in the cleaning section. Rinse under running water and allow to dry in a warm place or use copper cleaner and dobbie pad then rinse well and dry before using. For a dish you will be using a kiln so put on your gauge mesh (which incidentally should be bent at right angles on two sides so that you can easily lift it in and out of the kiln on a spatula) and place it in the kiln until it is a dull red. Remove, cool then clean in pickle, followed by rinsing and a good scrub with fine steel wool and detergent before thoroughly rinsing again. Placing on top of the kiln will hasten drying.

Whichever method you use, always hold by the edges to avoid any fingermarks on the surface as these could affect the adherence of the enamel.

APPLICATION

Cut a number of squares of a nylon stocking, if of a coarse mesh use double, and with small rubber bands stretch tightly over the mouth of each glass container (never keep your enamel powder in metal containers, it deteriorates). This acts as a convenient sieve to evenly spread your enamels, and it is very easy to slip off to return powder after use. The plastic lids will fit over the top of the stocking if you wish. Never leave uncovered as the powder will become damp and lumpy. Some people prefer to use small sized fine mesh sieves but I find the stocking covered containers very handy.

SGRAFFITO

This is simple and effective. Fire the background colour (black), cool, clean off the fire scale and place on paper. Cover with white in an even coat. Using a toothpick or the end of a match according to the width of line you require, scratch a pattern through to the black background. Children love this as it is a simple way to put their names on jewellery pieces.

If working this method on a large piece, a bowl or plate, it is necessary to have an adhesive of some kind — Gum Tragacanth (commonly called Gum Trag), oil of lavender, or Glycerine are all good, but when using them leave the piece to dry thoroughly before firing. Moisture will make your enamel bubble, the oil of lavender fumes will catch fire and ruin the colours.

The easiest way to put Gum Trag onto a bowl is to spray with a thin solution, working on a section at a time, from the top edge to the bottom on the inside, and from the bottom to the edge on the outside. After completely covering in powder, spray another coat of Gum Trag to hold it. Stilts or trivets must be used if you are counter-enamelling a bowl or another piece. When you remove it from the kiln and while it is still dull red, lift off with a flat file or similar instrument and place on asbestos to cool. This will leave either three little bare spots, or three pulled threads of enamel where the article was resting on the spikes. The spots aren't important, after all they are on the back, the little pulled threads can be filed down to neaten. If working a design on a bowl or a plate where the enamel has been over-sprayed with Gum Trag and allowed to dry before scratching in the pattern, it is possible to remove the excess with a soft brush. However, it can be left in and forms a slightly raised texture when fired.

Beads, threads, etc. can be included with a second coat of enamel to hold them in place. However, if you are satisfied with the finish of the base coat, then paint on some Gum Trag to hold them in position or they will roll off the edge, or the heat will cause them to jump off.

Gum Trag can be bought ready mixed in a jelly form which has an additive to prevent deterioration. However, some people prefer to mix their own. Mix 1 teaspoon of tragacanth powder and 1 tablespoon of methylated spirits to form a paste and pour immediately into 1 pint of water (preferably distilled), stirring all the time. Then put into a screw top jar and shake vigorously. Add 3 to 5 drops of soapless household detergent and Dettol or similar to prevent it 'going off'. Leave to stand overnight and then pour off liquid.

DECORATION

You can buy coloured beads of enamel in separate or mixed colours, opaque, transparent, or mixed, lumps of frit, threads in a variety of thicknesses, all of which add interest to your designs. You can also use paper stencils, negative or positive, hair-net (the heavy kind), wire mesh, the skeleton of a dead leaf — the possibilities are endless. Always fire a base coat of background colour before adding anything in the way of decoration and also, fire between separate colours or your powders will become hopelessly mixed. Remember that two colours mixed do not make a third colour.

ENAMELLING WITH A GAS TORCH
Requirements
Gas torch, large or medium end; tripod; stainless steel gauze; glass containers of enamel powder with stocking and rubber bands fitted on top; lumps; beads; threads; gum trag; oil of lavender; paint brush; tool for scratching design; clean paper;

spatula or cake slice for lifting hot piece; steel wool; or copper cleaner and dobbie pad for cleaning off the back; copper blank.

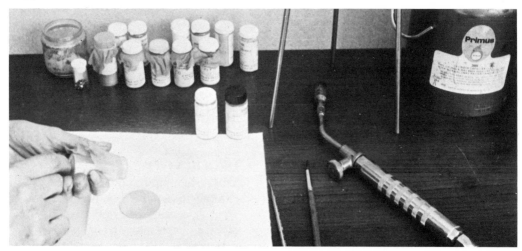

Step 1. After thoroughly cleaning the copper, place it on paper and sprinkle evenly with powder.

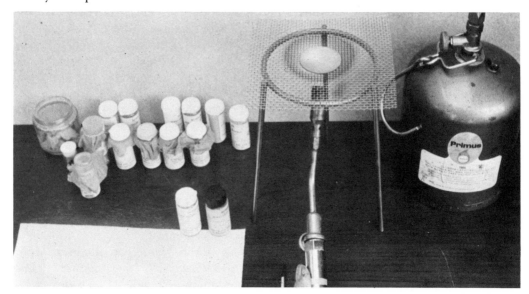

Step 2. Heat with the tip of a blue flame, rotating gently until glowing red. Clean fire scale from the back when cool.

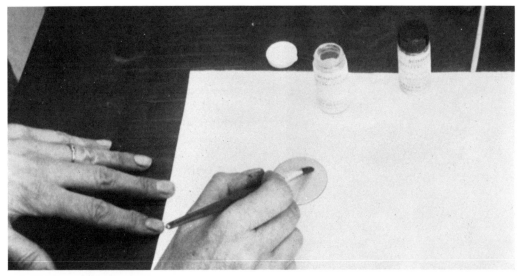

Step 3. Paint with gum trag and place a cut paper stencil on it.

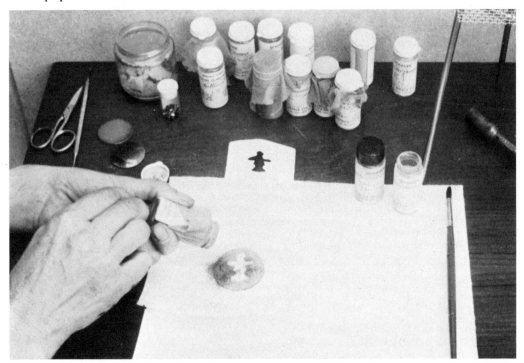

Step 4. Add contrasting coloured enamel and a few beads. Carefully remove stencil.

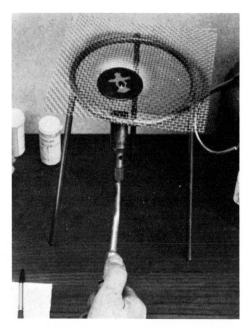

Step 5. Re-fire until glowing red. Cool and clean. File edges back to copper for a neat finish.

A hanger can be glued to the back with resin or if a hole is required to take a jump ring do it before you start enamelling.

ENAMELLED JEWELLERY SET IN BLACK, WHITE AND RED
(See photograph on page 66)
Requirements
Findings, silver coloured; satin finished steel surround for pendant; matching ring, bracelet links and clip fastening; pair of ear-ring clips; jump rings; chain. Copper blanks: 1 round to swing inside pendant; small round for ring; 6 bracelet shape; 3 triangles for pendant; 2 for ear-rings; enamel; opaque glossy black, red enamel powder, white and red beads.

1. Clean the copper blanks thoroughly with fine steel wool then vinegar and salt, rinse well and dry.
2. Enamel the ring blank red, the rest black. Remove the fire scale. Cover the pendant centre blank and the bracelet pieces with an even coat of white and with a sharp tool (a compass point or dental probe) scratch a series of lines from almost the centre out to the edges on each piece so that the black base coat shows through the white powder.
3. With a small pair of tweezers, position the red enamel beads across the centre of each piece, pressing slightly so that they will not roll off.
4. Re-fire, clean off the fire scale and assemble. As all the pieces are small this set could be done with either a gas torch or a kiln.

ENAMELLING WITH A KILN
An electric kiln is an expensive item, both to buy and to run but it makes enamelling a real pleasure once you are used to it. If you decide to invest in one, buy a good one even if it means saving a little longer. While there are small cheap ones on the market their use is limited and you will soon outgrow them and long for something more versatile.

As well as your kiln, you will need one or more asbestos sheets on which to place the hot mesh and enamelled pieces when you lift them out. This photo was taken of a school kiln which is why the asbestos is a little the worse for wear. You will also see how to bend the mesh.

Four wooden ornaments featuring a continuous enamelled design and copper wire as an added dimension.

Enamelling with a kiln.

Next to the mesh in the photograph is a small spatula. Use this to pick up the copper piece after the enamel powder has been shaken up. Slip the square corner under first — this will prevent you from picking up the excess powder at the same time. If this gets on the mesh it will either melt onto the back of the piece of copper and have to be filed off, or fall onto the floor of the kiln interior and in time this will be ruined. A metal egg slice makes a good tool for lifting in and out of the kiln. Next to this is a pointed utensil from a barbecue set which I bent at the end at right angles to form an excellent swirling tool. If you have a handyman to do it for you, a dental probe fitted into a long handle is even better for swirling.

Swirling This is done when the piece in the kiln is glowing red. With the point of the tool swirl the beads and/or threads into patterns. Work with all possible speed as the temperature drops and the enamel stiffens, sticks to the tool and drags off. Close the kiln door again for a few seconds so that the surface smooths out.

Actually, swirling is more easily done when using a gas torch because you can maintain the heat and also see exactly what you are doing.

To the left of the glass tubes of enamel powder is gum trag, oil of lavender and glycerine, any of which can be used as adhesives. Behind these you will see a stainless steel trivet on which you must rest a counter-enamelled piece while you are working on the right side, otherwise it will stick to the mesh. In the small covered plastic bucket is copper cleaner and dobbie pad for cleaning off fire scale. Steel wool is suitable for quickly removing the loose pieces between firings but for the final cleaning or to clean up burnt back edges (caused by too little enamel powder or too much heat) so that they can be re-done, copper cleaner is the answer. Incidentally, if you are doing a repair job on the edges, after cleaning, rinsing well and drying, paint with one of the adhesives, add the powder and be sure to dry before firing.

In the foreground is the top for a box in three pieces of 18g. copper each 6in x 2½in making 15 x 19 cm overall. They have already had the edges filed and smoothed, been thoroughly cleaned, counter-enamelled and given two coats each of glossy black base colour. **Remember** you must now use a trivet on the mesh every time you fire one of these counter-enamelled pieces.

Step 1. Draw a suitable design for a stencil and cut it out neatly with a Gem blade or a cutting knife. Dampening the paper helps to avoid spilling the excess powder. Dip the stencil in water and blot it between

This design is built up from wire and nails and makes an amazing wall hanging. (See page 100 for instructions.)

two paper towels then lay it carefully in position, making sure the enamelled pieces are close together and lined up exactly. Take the opaque white (or any choice of colour) with its stocking mesh on top (hold it so that any spare stocking does not drag in the powder as you apply it) and tapping sharply on the bottom, work around the stencil so that you have a fairly thick coat at the edge of the paper tapering out onto the black.

Step 2. Carefully remove the stencil. If any grains of powder fall where you don't want them, pick them up with a damp paint brush so that the pattern is clear and sharp. An easy way to pick up a stencil if you are nervous about it, is with one or two strips of Scotch tape pressed onto the surface where it is free from powder. Fire one piece at a time with the trivet to support them on the mesh. As soon as you remove a fired piece from the kiln and while it is still dull red, slip a flat file under and lift off the trivet onto the asbestos. Any little 'pulls' can be filed smooth when cool. Apart from not warping the copper, counter-enamelling means you don't have to clean the back between firings.

When the three pieces are cool re-assemble on the paper for the next step.

Step 3. Using the soft brush and one of the adhesives paint a free hand over-pattern to add a bit of interest. Shake on a liberal amount of contrasting colour, in this case it was leaf green. Holding the work over a fresh sheet of paper and taking one piece at a time, turn over and tap sharply on the back with your fingers. The excess enamel powder which has not adhered to the oil will fall off. Put aside in a warm place, e.g. the top of the kiln, to dry.

Note: It is most important that you do not fire before the work is perfectly dry or the fumes from the oil of lavender will catch fire in the kiln and ruin both the colour and the finish. If you are in a desperate hurry it is possible to hasten the drying process by placing a piece at a time on the mesh and, with the door of the kiln open, passing it in and out quickly a few times.

When the firing has been completed clean the edges with a small file so that the copper shows up brightly and lacquer with a small brush so that it will not tarnish later. I used a strong box which had originally contained cigars. The inside was painted flat green to match the colour in the design and the outside sprayed with several coats of glossy black. The enamelled pieces were attached with contact cement.

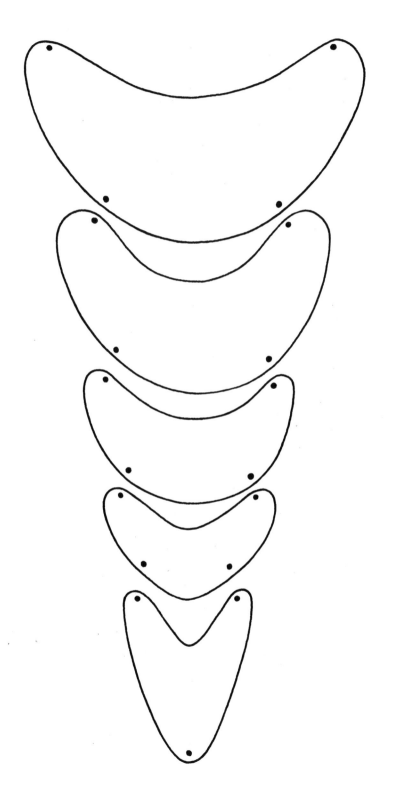

INSTRUCTIONS FOR ENAMELLED NECKLACE

(See photograph on page 75.)

Requirements

20 gauge sheet copper; 6 mm jump rings; Lengths of chain (fine for tassel); Coarse hairnet for patterning.

Diagram on previous page shows the size to cut your five shapes. Smooth the edges using your small half-round file followed by fine steel wool. Drill the holes to take the jump rings and smooth off any burrs. Clean all over with the steel wool then copper cleaner and dobbie pad. Rinse well and dry.

Note: When putting on the enamel, arrange the pieces together on a large sheet of paper and work on them all at the same time. This is specially important when doing the pattern with the hairnet so that it will all match. Fire separately with a gas torch or in groups in the kiln.

When the colour and finish of the base coats are to your satisfaction assemble again, wet the hairnet, squeeze out excess moisture and drape it over so that it forms a nice pattern.

Spread over a liberal amount of opaque enamel powder and carefully remove the net. Re-fire. Clean the edges with a file, backs with copper cleaner and lacquer if desired to keep the copper bright. Join together with the jump rings. Add a short chain, make a fastening hook with wire and make a tassel by cutting fine chain into lengths and attach.

Geometrical genius

There is a growing interest at present in the fascinating pastime of building designs with nails and string, cotton, wool etc. on boards. Have you considered the wonderful effects possible with fine wire?

The beauty of this hobby is that you require the very minimum of equipment: pineboard (at least 1.3 cm thick); panel pins; a hammer; a ruler and pencil; paint, felt or hessian to cover the board, and the stringing material. I prefer wire for this, naturally, because it is bright and subtly changes colour with the angle of light. Readily available by the reel at radio and electrical suppliers' shops, copper wire is in several different colours, for example, 30 gauge is a deep copper colour, 36 gauge is a very light copper shade and by varying these you get a very interesting result.

* *Board with graduated nails, all painted black, being strung in two colours of copper wire, 30 gauge and 36 gauge, which is bought by the reel.*

Choose a piece of board the size you require and work out a geometrical design to fit it. Two straight lines drawn at an angle to each other, marked out to have an equal number of nails in each, and strung together, will give you a design with a curved edge. The only thing to remember is that you string 1 to 1, 2 to 2, etc. (Fig 1.)

With a design which has long lines with short lines then the nails must be positioned closer together on the short side in order to have a corresponding number. (Fig 2.)

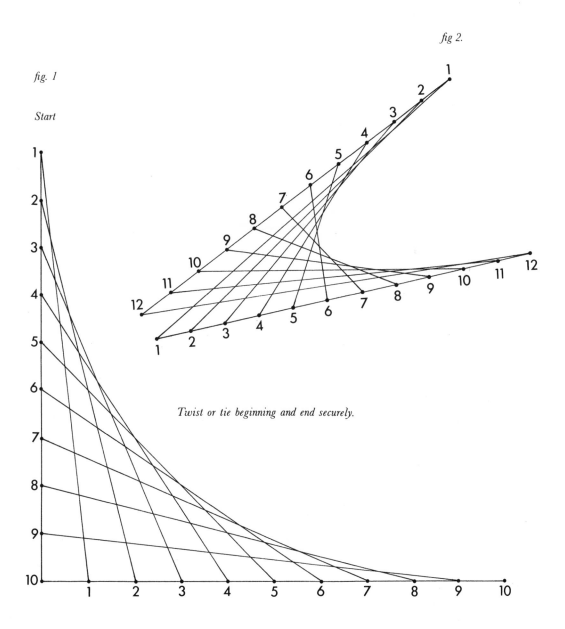

fig 2.

fig. 1

Start

Twist or tie beginning and end securely.

By varying the height of the panel pins, for example in fig 3, leave 2 cm panel pins high in the middle and hammered as low as possible (without coming through the back of the board) at the edge or by using smaller ones at the ends, a more 3D effect can be obtained. It is then possible, by having the nails higher, to add a design which overlays the first part but doesn't touch it.

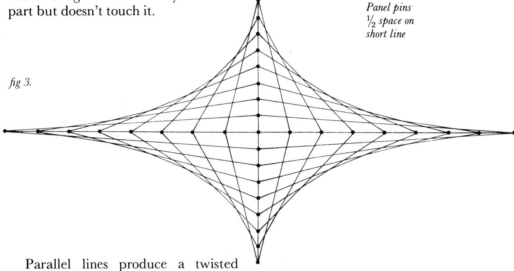

fig 3.

Panel pins
½ space on
short line

Parallel lines produce a twisted effect. (Fig 4.)

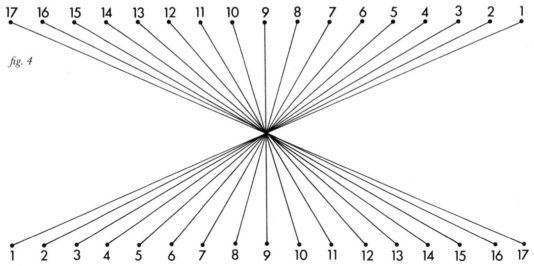

fig. 4

A circle or half circle is worked by
taking the thread from nail one to the
first nail past half way. (Fig 5.)

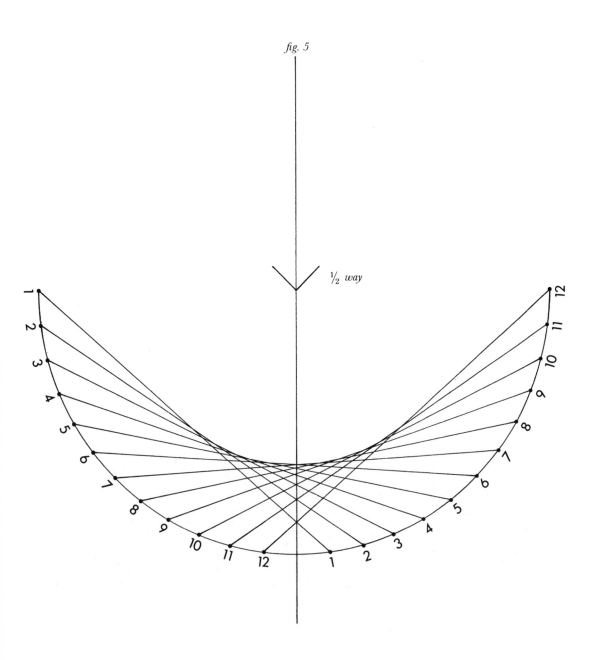

fig. 5

½ *way*

Another very pretty effect will result if a complete circle is worked in several colours.

fig 6.

wire round peg

Board

By adding a peg (a piece of fine dowel, meat skewer or wooden knitting needle) to a point in your design you can build it progressively higher by taking the wire round the peg each time you pass from one nail to the opposite one. (Fig 6.)

You have several choices on how to finish the board itself.

1. Draw the design onto the board which has been sanded smooth. Measure accurately and hammer in the nails to the required height. Paint or spray-paint the board and the nails. Don't forget the edges of the board. Allow to dry thoroughly before starting the design.

2. Cover the board with hessian. Cut hessian to fit the board plus about 7 cm all around to fold over the edges and fasten on the back. Spread Aquadhere evenly over the board and edges, lay the hessian on and smooth it out so that it is tight and wrinkle free. Turn face down and glue to the back. Allow to dry.

Draw the design on paper with the position for nails marked. Pin to the board and hammer the nails in through the paper. While the paper design is still on the board paint the nails a colour to match the hessian. This not only stops the nails from rusting, but also they are not clear enough if painted the same colour as the background. When dry tear away the paper.

3. Felt can be used in the same manner as hessian. If you wish to add a peg, drill a hole for it after you have covered the background but before you paint the nails as it must be painted too.

Board covered with felt showing different heights of nails and peg after painting and removing paper design.

Note: Coloured hessian and felt in many bright shades can be bought in craft or hobby shops or in most big department stores. Panel pins (fine nails will small heads) are available in hardware stores. Buy a packet, you will use more than you would think.

You are now ready to wire the design according to your plan. Be sure to secure the beginnings and endings by winding the wire round a panel pin and then back on itself so that it cannot come undone.

Note: Keep a firm tension on the wire at all times or it will soon begin to sag.

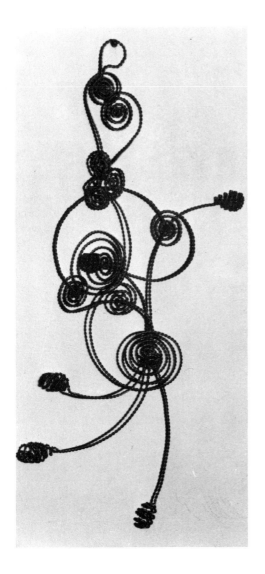
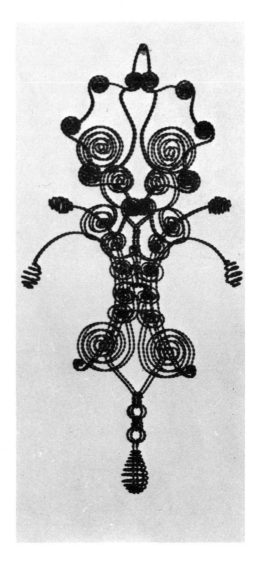

WIRE SCULPTURE

Eight gauge or ten gauge soft copper rod can be bent quite easily even with the fingers to form abstract figures. Sketch a design, enlarge to the size required and use this as a guide. Lie the rod on top of the line drawing and just keep bending. When the number of figures you want have been formed, they can be mounted by fixing the wires which form the legs into a block of cork, or driftwood, or a shape cast in plaster or resin. They will push easily into cork, but for other materials drill appropriate sized holes and glue them in with epoxy resin, wood cement or a similar product. Refer to the chapter on twisting wire with a drill. A heavy gauge wire makes a more impressive decoration for a wall.

In the photograph on page 111, which is just a flowing shape, 18 gauge wire is twisted by hand. No solder was used. The shapes just link together.

Plus perspex

Perspex shapes, which are made by mixing together liquid embedding casting resin and polyester hardener and pouring it into moulds to set, add colour and dimension to your copper plaques, doors and sculptural forms. It can be tinted by stirring in coloured inks or liquid dyes, either during mixing or quickly after pouring onto moulds. (Ink from the plastic inside of a Biro gives brilliant colours.) Pieces of crushed or broken coloured glass (amber from beer bottles, green from wine bottles) glass beads or marbles, scraps of copper or coiled wire add further interest.

Setting in glass gives a beautifully smooth surface, any household glass which is wider at the mouth than the sides and base will serve, my best stemmed sweet dishes often get used, also champagne glasses with solid stems. A lot of heat is generated during the setting process but when solid, the shape shrinks and makes removal easy. Any drips which may adhere to the glass can be removed by soaking in very hot water. If you are worried, a mould release wax is available but furniture wax rubbed on and then polished off with a soft cloth will suffice. However, given time, or a little extra heat after setting (put in the oven at 150° F for half an hour) the shrinkage will be sufficient. Any geometrical shape other than a sphere can be made in heavy cardboard. The joins can be well strapped with masking tape, sealed with lacquer and then used as a mould.

Heavy plastic or glass moulds can be bought, also glass spheres in two sizes. These are in very thin glass with a pouring neck. After setting, shatter the glass by tapping it gently. This material is very versatile, it can be sawn, filed, drilled and highly polished.

Note: This product has been developed for the home handyman but precaution should be taken. It is flammable and the hardener is poisonous. Use strictly as directed on the tin, in a well-ventilated area, do not smoke, or inhale the fumes.

Polishing

Should the surface be rough it can be filed, then rubbed with various grades of 'wet and dry', preferably under running water. When the shape feels smooth the surface will look cloudy but this can be corrected by rubbing well with toothpaste on a damp cloth. Finish with Brasso and a soft cloth for a high shine. For shapes set in glass polishing with Brasso is generally sufficient.

WALL CLOCK IN ENAMEL AND PERSPEX

Requirements

Cut or buy twelve shapes in 18-20 gauge copper, to substitute for numbers and enamel them. By using the same base colour on each, you will achieve continuity. (If you wish to add numbers or Roman numerals you could cut them in copper wire, square wire or sheet copper and set them into the enamel but remember to lacquer after polishing off the fire scale); a turned copper bowl, 11.4 cm diameter. Drill a hole in the centre large enough to fit over the shaft which carries the hands and enamel in colours to match, on the outside only; a

battery-operated clock movement, this can be bought from a jeweller, or use one from an old clock; embedding casting resin; scales and plastic ice-cream container; polyester hardener; plastic medicine glass for measurement; a few drops of melted paraffin wax; a round cake or biscuit tin lid to use as a mould; wax to release; cardboard, masking tape, lacquer; metal hanger and small screws; resin; weight.

1. Measure the case of the clock movement and make an exact replica of the outside dimensions with cardboard and masking tape. Give two coats of lacquer and allow to dry thoroughly.
2. Wax the tin lid and polish well.
3. Place the clock movement in the lid and measure carefully so that the axis of the hands is exactly in the centre. Mark round the edge.
4. Replace the movement with the

cardboard shape and stand something heavy inside it so that it cannot move out of position.

5. Place the ice-cream container (½gal size) on the scales and measure 1 lb (450 g) of casting resin and add the melted paraffin wax. In the plastic medicine glass measure 5 ml of polyester hardener (more or less according to the weather, read the instructions on the bottle).

Note: Remember to allow for the weight of the container. Resin attracts moisture from the air and the surface is inclined to stay sticky. The addition of the paraffin wax prevents this and gives a hard, easy-to-polish surface, so try not to forget it.

Stir quickly, pour into the mould. It should be about 1.3 mm thick over all. The amount required will depend on the diameter of the lid. If not thick enough estimate how much you will need and immediately mix some more and pour in.

6. Allow to set hard — at least one day. Remove the weight, the mould and then the cardboard shape. Polish.

7. Take the hands from the clock movement and fit it into the space. If too tight, file a little off the perspex but remember the fit needs to be firm.

8. Fit the hole in the inverted bowl over the shaft and try the hands to ensure that the clearance is right and that the bowl edge lies on the perspex. Adjust the clock movement until it is correct. The edge of the bowl can be attached to the perspex with resin

if you wish, but if everything fits correctly it will all hold together.

9. Carefully position the enamelled pieces for the numbers, attach with Araldite and clamp in place until set.

10. Add the hanger to the upper back of the perspex by drilling with a fine bit and screwing securely.

11. Replace the hands, put in the battery and hang on your wall.

Opposite:
A startlingly effective and simple primitive sculpture in copper wire buried in cork. This is an ideal beginning for the young coppercraft convert. (See page 106 for instructions.)

Overleaf:
An etched printing plate, here mounted for a wall-hanging. This design can then be printed on paper. (See page 119 for instructions.)

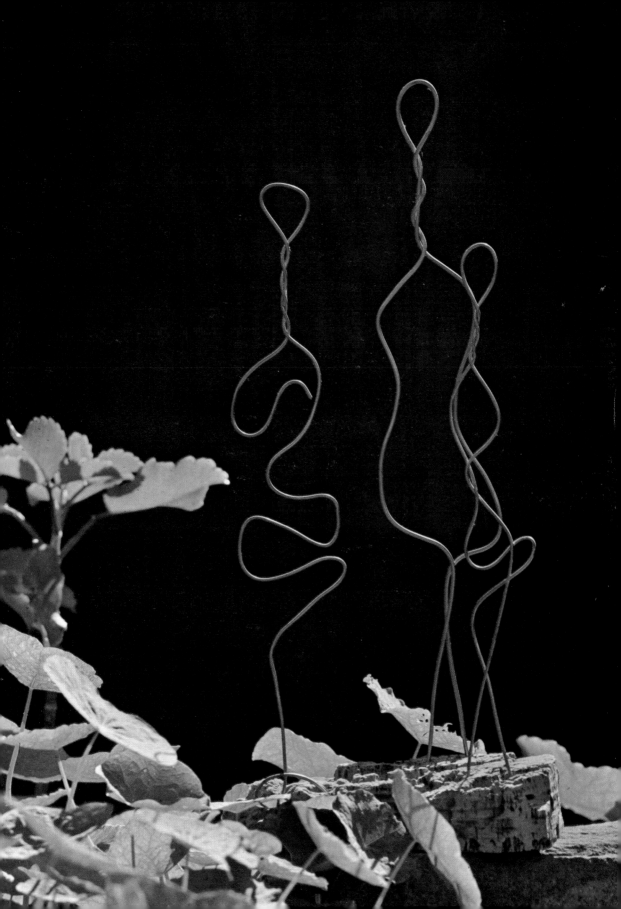

Etching and printing

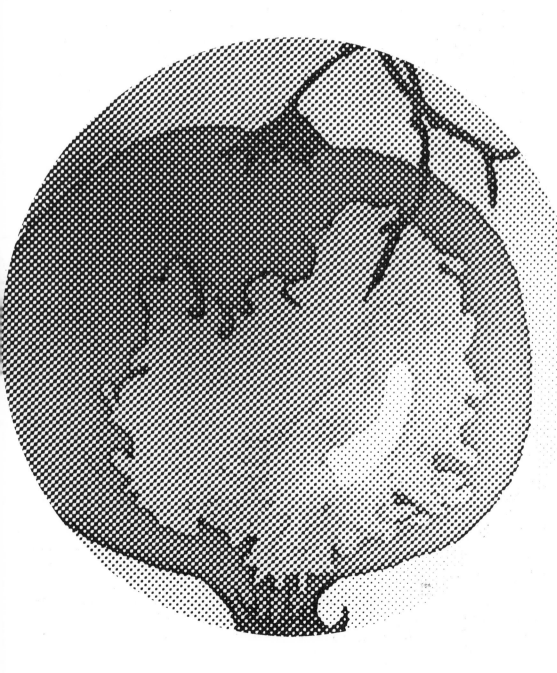

Intaglio Printing is printing from an engraved, incised or etched line on the surface of a design. The image to be printed is cut into the surface of a copper (or zinc) plate and filled with printing ink. The plate is then wiped clean so that the ink remains only in the incised areas. Damp paper under great pressure is pressed into the ink as the paper passes between the two rollers of an Intaglio press.

As many schools have equipment which could be used if teachers knew what to do with it, I decided that a section on etching and printing could be of valuable assistance. Once you have mastered the etching processes as described for jewellery and dishes, etching a copper plate for printing purposes will present no real difficulties. I was very fortunate to have had as an instructress Elizabeth Rooney who is well known for the quality of her prints. The following notes were given to me by her and included here with her kind permission.

Note: Asphaltum is referred to as Stop-out varnish. The inclusion of instructions for zinc plates is incidental.

Requirements

1. Acid bath big enough to take the plates you wish to use.
2. Etching agent. Commercial Nitric Acid: 2 parts water plus 1 part acid for copper; 12 parts water plus 1 part acid for zinc.
3. Running water and good ventilation are essential.
4. Hot plate for heating copper plates when using 'grounds', Aquatint, and for warming the plates before applying the printing ink.
5. Suitable metal; copper or zinc are the best, 16-20 gauge.
6. File, large, for bevelling the edges of the plate. This means to file the four edges to a 45° angle towards the front (or image side) of the plate so that it will not cut the printing blankets or the paper.
7. 'Wet and Dry' 500 and 600 or Bon Ami and water to get a good surface on the plate; vinegar and salt to clean the copper; ammonia and whiting to remove the grease which is always on metal, before applying 'ground'.

Note: Never use vinegar to clean zinc.

8. Ground. This is a compound of beeswax, bitumen and resin which is used on the image side of the plate. You can buy Hard Ground or Soft Ground. Soft ground is Hard ground mixed with an equal quantity of grease. It is applied to a clean heated plate with the aid of a dabber which can be made by tightly rolling a nylon stocking and tying it to form a mushroom shape.
9. Stop-out varnish (Asphaltum) to be applied to the underside of plates before etching commences and also for blocking out areas on the image side when using the Aquatint process; brushes and solvents; Mineral Turps for removing Stop-out varnish; Methylated Spirit for removing resin in Aquatinting.
10. String to lower the plates into the acid bath. Feathers to remove the bubbles during the etching.
11. Intaglio Press, printing blankets (also referred to as felts); cardboard handling clips (these are pieces of cardboard about 2.5 cm x 10 cm

folded in half and used to lift paper or blankets when your fingers are inky).

12. Copperplate printing ink and dabber for applying it to the etched plate. A dabber can be made by tightly rolling calico or cotton material to about 3 cm x 10 cm long and tying securely. This is used to push the ink down into the etched design on the warmed printing plate. Stiff book muslin is then used to wipe the surface of the plate to remove the surplus ink. The final wiping of the plate is done with the palm of the hand. Use hand paste to protect the skin. (Ink should be in the design only, not on the face of the plate when printing commences.)

13. Esparto cartridge paper or mould-made 120lb or hand-made etching paper. Tissue paper for storing the prints.

14. Scriber, pencil, airmail paper for designs. A ruler and two match boxes to make a hand rest. When putting a design on either hard or soft ground never rest your hand on the plate as this could damage the surface.

free from scratches and flaws as possible. Thoroughly clean both sides with 'Wet and Dry' 500 and 600 or Bon Ami, water and a soft cloth. This will reveal any deep scratches or pits. Select the best side for your design, this is called the image side. If you are lucky you will have a perfect surface, but for marks that may detract from the final print several methods can be tried which should smooth them out. The tools are relatively cheap.

1. Snake stone and water

2. Scraping (dry)

3. Burnishing (+ *oil*)

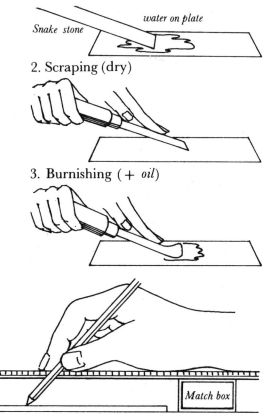

Preparing the plate

No matter which etching process you intend to use, Asphaltum or Hard or Soft ground, the initial preparation is the same. Choose a piece of copper as

Any roughness on the surface of the image side will catch the ink and show on the print as a dirty mark. Sometimes this can be used to advantage, e.g. on the pomegranate prints a few remaining scratches added a little interest to an otherwise rather large background, but as a general rule it is better to remove them if possible.

With the file, bevel the edges of the plate towards the image side. Any roughness left by the file can be smoothed off with 'Wet and dry'. Clean the plate thoroughly on both sides with vinegar and salt, rinse well, dry and proceed with whichever method you have decided to use, depending on the end result you require. Soft ground is for soft looking lines and textured patterns, hard ground gives sharp precise lines and lends itself to cross-hatched type shading, while Asphaltum is best for designs where progressive stopping-out is required to give graduating tones. The process called Aquatint can be used in conjunction with any of these methods to add extra tonal areas.

HARD GROUND ETCHING

Take your prepared plate and clean the image side with ammonia and whiting, rinse well and dry. This can be hastened by putting in a warm place or by a fan. Heat the plate gently and with the hard ground 'knob' press spots onto the warmed metal.

Using the dabber spread onto an even film all over the surface. When the ground has cooled and set hold the plate at an angle over a taper or candle and smoke the surface until the sooty look disappears and a shiny black appearance results. This gives extra hardness. Cool again.

Paint the back and edges with Asphaltum and allow to dry, then secure your design with Scotch tape and using the hand rest, trace round with a Biro or needle so that the impression will show on the hard ground surface.

With a scriber (or needle) scratch through the surface but do not dig into the metal. Holding the plate in a loop of string lower it into the prepared acid bath. Lie the ends of the string over the edges of the bath and use it to lift the plate out again when the etching needs checking or is finished. With the feather remove the bubbles from the surface of the plate as they form.

When the etch is deep enough remove from the acid. Rinse well under running water, remove the hard ground and Asphaltum with turpentine and polish with Brasso. It is now ready for the printing ink. (See page 120 for printing from the etched plate.)

SOFT GROUND ETCHING

The application of soft ground to your plate is basically the same as for hard ground except that it is not smoked. Make a fresh dabber, never interchange them.

Substituting a soft ground knob follow the previous instructions until you have an even film all over the surface. Allow to cool.

Paint the back and edges with Asphaltum and allow to dry. Draw your design on airmail weight paper, place on the plate, and using the hand rest draw round with an H or HB pencil. The soft ground will adhere to the back of the paper with the pressure of the pencil and when lifted off will leave the design imprinted on the surface.

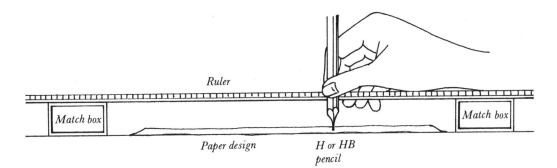

Ruler

Match box

Paper design

H or HB
pencil

Match box

The plate can now be etched, or a texture can be added by using material with an interesting weave; lace, string, in fact anything that is not hard or sharp as these would damage the printing equipment. Place the plate image side up on the bed of the press, place texture pieces on in the required pattern, cover with a sheet of grease-proof paper then an old printing blanket. Imprint the texture into the soft ground surface by putting this through the press at two thirds the normal pressure for printing. Any areas you then decide to eliminate can be masked out with Asphaltum before putting in the acid bath.

Very interesting effects can be achieved in this way. After etching and cleaning the plate run off a trial print. If darker areas are desired treat with Aquatint and stop-out varnish and re-etch.

AQUATINT

When etching with hard or soft ground or stop-out varnish the tonal strength of lines is determined by the length of time the plate is exposed to the acid. As Nitric acid slightly undermines the surface of the metal, heavy lines for dark areas should be spaced further apart than the light

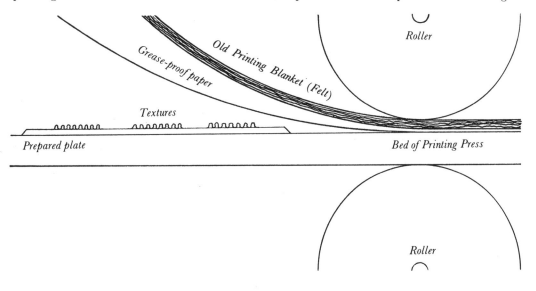

Roller

Grease-proof paper

Old Printing Blanket (Felt)

Textures

Prepared plate

Bed of Printing Press

Roller

lines which are blocked out after a shorter exposure. Aquatint is a quicker process for gaining tonal effect but is less durable, i.e. it would last for a limited number of prints only. However, this would not be a disadvantage for a classroom or hobbyist.

Powdered resin is tied in a square of silk or nylon, held over a clean dry cold etched plate, and tapped with the fingers so that a film of resin particles falls on the surface. When heated gently on the hot plate these particles melt onto the plate, sealing it against the action of the acid. (When melted they look clear like tiny drops of water.) If too much resin is used the acid cannot penetrate and there will be no etch, but if not enough there will be too much etch so check the plate before heating.

Note: Always use a single piece of newspaper under your plate for easy moving, big enough to hold by the sides like a sling. This facilitates moving it on and off the hot plate without putting your fingers on the surface, or burning yourself. An etched plate with the Asphaltum still on the back and/or image side can be aquatinted if you are very careful not to overheat. The newspaper will prevent it sticking to the hot plate.

Any tonal quality from pale grey to deep black can be achieved with Aquatint depending on the depth of the etch between the particles. As the resultant colour depends on the amount of printing ink trapped in the roughened surface, a slight roughness (a light etch), will give a light tone. Progressively dark shades of tone can be done simply by repeatedly removing the plate from the acid bath, washing, drying, stopping out areas on which you judge etch to be sufficient, and then returning to the acid. In this way the lighter areas are protected until the darkest areas are deep enough. In the same way, after the resin has been melted onto the plate any areas you do not wish to be toned at all are blocked out with Asphaltum before putting into the acid the first time.

Aquatint Tonal Areas are etched through a layer of powdered resin particles which are dusted onto a clean dry cold plate, and then melted by heating gently. Powdered resin in a piece of silk or nylon held over the plate and tapped with the fingers so that a film of particles covers the surface in an even layer. Too much resin will give no etch and too little resin gives too much etch so check before heating!

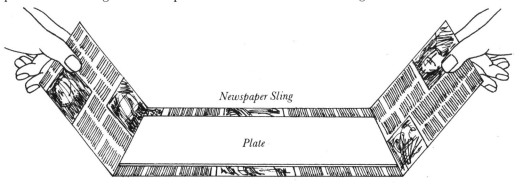

Newspaper Sling

Plate

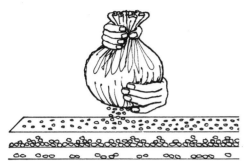

When the Aquatint process has been completed to your satisfaction remove the resin from the plate with Methylated spirit, the Asphaltum with Turpentine, and polish the whole plate carefully with Brasso. It is now ready for printing.

Note: For any of the etching processes, Dutch Mordant, which gives a slow fine etch, can be used as an alternative to Nitric Acid. It is made by boiling together 2 parts of Potassium Chlorate with a little water until dissolved, adding 70 parts water and 10 parts concentrated Hydrochloric Acid and stirring well. Allow to stand for 24 hours before using. Remember that it will take a longer time to produce the same result.

ETCHING WITH STOP-OUT VARNISH (ASPHALTUM)

(See photograph on page 112)
For the following etched printing plate I used a 30 cm x 30 cm square of 16 gauge copper. By progressively stopping out areas of the design during etching I was able to achieve a gradation of tone. I used the Aquatint process for the darkest parts, i.e. the stem and base.

Having drawn my design I carefully cleaned and prepared the plate as previously described, bevelling the edges and removing all

but the most stubborn scratches (which in the end result in this case did not spoil the effect). The back was painted with Asphaltum and allowed to dry. The design was applied with carbon paper, the lines remained visible through the progressive stages and were a guide for each additional application of stop-out.

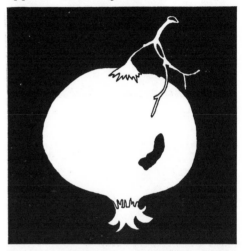

Step 1. Asphaltum over the whole background, edges, and two highlights. Etch, rinse well, dry.

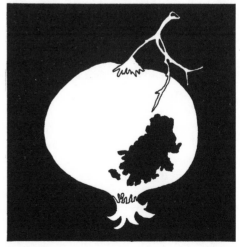

Step 2. Block out next level of the design. Etch, rinse and dry as before.

Step 3. Repeat the process for the next level.

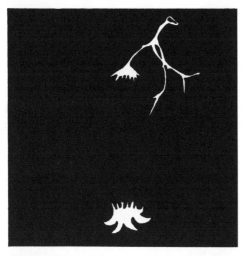

Step 4. Aquatint and etch the stem and base for the darkest tone. Careful heating will not effect the Asphaltum. Etch the desired amount, rinse and clean.

Having removed the resin and stop-out with Methylated Spirit and turpentine, carefully polish with Brasso ready for printing.

After I had used the plate for printing, I polished it with Brasso again, sealed the surface with several coats of metal lacquer (50-50 with thinners) mounted it on a square of pineboard and hung it as a group with the framed prints.

PRINTING FROM THE ETCHED PLATE

1. Prepare the paper well in advance, 24 hours if possible. Soak in water, flat, until saturated, then store (still flat) in plastic sheeting. Before using, remove any excess water by pressing each sheet between two pieces of blotting paper.

2. Thoroughly clean the etched plate of all ground, Asphaltum or resin, give the image side a final polish with Brasso and a soft cloth.

3. Adjust the printing pressure before inking the etched plate. Place the plate on the bed of the press, a double sheet of prepared paper (always use two sheets together for best results) over the plate, then lay the printing blankets over all. Loosen the pressure screws to nil resistance on the first run, return to the point where the blankets and paper are under the roller, turn screws evenly till they stop but do not tighten. A firm even pressure for a clear even print should be the result of the test run. Although no ink has been used a clear imprint of the design should show as the damp paper surface has been pressed into the etch.

4. Warm the etched plate, apply the printing ink with the rolled cotton dabber pushing it into the design with a circular movement. Wipe as much excess ink as possible off the face of the plate wth a crumpled piece of book muslin, and finish off by wiping with the palm of the hand (previously protected with a little hand paste).

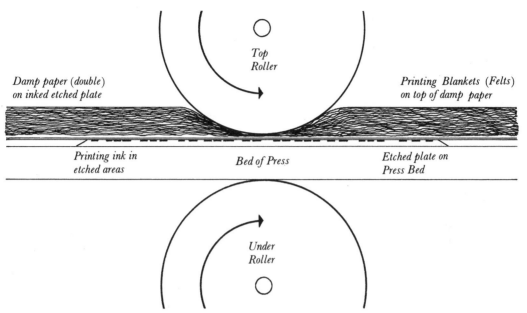

Damp paper (double)
on inked etched plate

Top Roller

Printing Blankets (Felts)
on top of damp paper

Printing ink in
etched areas

Bed of Press

Etched plate on
Press Bed

Under Roller

When ready for printing the ink should be in the etched areas only, not on the background or highlights of the design.

5. Warm the plate again slightly before placing on the bed of the press.

6. Position the double paper carefully on top so the print will be centred.

7. Lie the blankets overall, turn the spindle of the press slowly and evenly for the full run. Using the cardboard handling clips, fold back the blankets and lift the print carefully from the plate.

8. Store wet prints carefully, preferably between sheets of tissue paper, wth a large sheet of cardboard both under and over to give a slight pressure while they are drying. Prints can be clipped to a line by two corners ·but if dried in this manner they will curl.

Do not be disappointed if the first few prints are not perfect. It generally takes several inkings before every tiny part of the etch becomes impregnated.

Remove the printing plate from the bed of the press, re-warm and repeat the inking and printing process until you are satisfied with the result.

There are a few rules to remember:—

1. Keep ink from the bed of the press and the blankets. Use the handling clips at all times when your fingers are inky.

2. When blankets become wet from contact with the damp paper change them or dry them before proceeding.

3. Never leave a printing plate dirty, when you ·have finished printing for the time being clean it thoroughly with turpentine and cotton waste. Before using it again polish it well with Brasso and a soft cloth to remove any oxidization that will have formed.

Glossary

ACID: Always treat with care. Add acid to water, never vice versa. Use in a well ventilated place.

ANNEALING: Heating copper until it is glowing red hot and then plunging in cold water to soften for easy working. Remove fire scale with pickle.

AQUATINT: Most effective method of etching wide areas of tone on a printing plate (for a limited edition of prints only). Powdered resin is sprinkled over the image side, fixed by careful heating, areas not to be toned are painted out with Asphaltum and then plate is put in acid bath. Roughened surface produced holds the printing ink and progressively darker tonal areas can be obtained by blocking out and re-etching. The deeper the etch the more ink it will hold.

ASPHALTUM: A bituminous paint used in etching to protect the design and back of article from action of acid. Sometimes called Block-Out Lacquer or Stop-Out Varnish.

BALL PEIN HAMMER: 113gm or 227gm suitable for copper work. Has one round end and one flat one. Round end can be used for texturing background of copper shim. Highly polished, either end can be used for planishing in sheet metal work.

BASSE-TAILLE: Completely covering an etched copper article with transparent enamel and firing. The greater depth in the etched areas gives a variation in colour.

BLANKS: Ready cut copper shapes, usually 18-19 gauge copper for enamelling or etching. Sizes from ear-ring or cuff-link up to turned bowls and plates, flat or shaped, are all called blanks.

BRIGHT DIP: 50-50 mixture of concentrated Nitric and Sulphuric acids with a pinch of common salt, used extensively in industry for shining copper and brass. Very dangerous for home use, NEVER for classroom use.

BURNISHING: Rubbing the surface of sheet copper with a burnishing tool and oil to close up pits and scratches when preparing the image side of a copper plate for etching.

BURR: Rough edge made when filing or machining metal. Rub smooth with fine steel wool or 'wet and dry' for a good finish. Enamel will shrink away from a burred edge on a bowl or plate because it holds grease.

CARBORUNDUM: Silicon carbide — a very hard abrasive. Can be bought as a stone, e.g. for rubbing enamel insets level with metal background in champlevé enamelling; or as 'wet and dry' paper, used for smoothing and polishing copper. Begin with 400, then 500 and finish with finest grade 600. Best used backwards and forwards rather than in a circular motion, to remove scratches.

CHAMPLEVE: Cutting a design into a surface of metal, e.g. by etching, then filling with enamel powders and firing so that a pattern of inlaid colours is achieved. Fire enamels, rub back so surrounding metal is clean, then re-fire. A very exacting process but very attractive when completed.

CLOISONNE: A French word meaning literally 'fenced in'. Partition areas of your design with copper wire (20-24 gauge, depending on the fineness you require) and fill these areas with different coloured enamel. When fired, enamels shrink so several firings are necessary to fill areas properly.

COPPERTONER: A preparation, a few drops in boiling water is used to oxidize copper by rubbing on with a soft cloth.

COUNTER ENAMEL: Enamelling both sides, this equalizes the strain and prevents the decorative enamel on the right side from cracking and chipping. Also gives a more finished appearance. A trivet must be used on the wire gauze when doing the second side to prevent sticking.

DABBER: (1) Mushroom shaped, made of nylon stocking, used for spreading an even layer of soft or hard ground over a warmed copper plate prior to etching. Keep separate dabbers for soft and hard, never interchange them. (2) Tight roll of cotton material about 2 cm diameter and 7 cm long securely tied and used to force printing ink down into the etched design on a warmed copper plate prior to wiping and printing.

DISCARDING ACID: When pickle or etching acid has become too weak to use, discard it by pouring slowly down a sink with a fast running tap, or neutralize it by gradually adding limestone, washing soda, or baking soda until no more reaction (bubbling) is seen then flush it away with plenty of water.

DOLLY: A polished steel shape with a flat base (like a stake without a shaft) used when flattening or shaping jewellery pieces with a ball pein hammer.

DUTCH MORDANT: A preparation used to produce a fine, slow etch. Boil

2 parts Potassium Chlorate with a little water until dissolved. Add 70 parts water and 10 parts concentrated Hydrochloric Acid.

ENAMEL: Is a vitreous glaze or glass coating fused onto metal by the use of heat 630-830°C according to the melting point of the particular one you are using.

ETCHING: To produce a design in the surface of copper by means of strokes, lines or areas being eaten down by a corrosive agent (nitric acid or Dutch Mordant) while protecting the rest of the surface by some form of block-out such as Asphaltum paint, hard or soft ground or Aquatint.

FINDINGS: These are really the finishings; cuff link and ear-ring fastenings, settings, rings with settings, bracelet links and catches, key-rings, jump rings, in fact everything you need to turn your enamelled pieces into usable articles. In bright copper or oxidized finish, non-tarnish.

FIRE BRICKS: Heat resistant bricks used to support copper when annealing or while soldering.

FIRE SCALE: Forms on copper when heat is applied. When heating copper to anneal, plunge in cold water to cool before putting into pickle to remove the fire scale. When the copper turns pink the surface will clean easily, rinse thoroughly under running water.

FRIT: Powdered glass used in enamel powder (also in pottery glazes).

GAUGE: The thickness of wire or sheet copper, the smaller the number, the thicker the material e.g. 28 gauge copper is very thin, 12 gauge is very heavy.

GROUND: Hard ground or soft ground — a combination of beeswax, resin and bitumen used for line etching.

IMAGE SIDE: The side of a copper printing plate which reveals the least blemishes after polishing, on which the design is then etched.

INTAGLIO PRINTING: Printing from an engraved, incised or etched line or design. The image to be printed is cut into the surface of a copper (or zinc) plate and filled with printing ink. The plate is then wiped clean so that the ink remains only in the incised area. Damp paper under great pressure is pressed into the ink as the plate passes between two rollers of an Intaglio press.

JUMP RINGS: Ready made fine wire rings in various sizes, bright copper or oxidized bought by the packet and used for links, e.g. to attach enamelled pendant to chain.

KILN: A small electric 'oven' for firing enamel. Buy the best you can afford for the type of work you wish to do. Open element kilns are not recommended, they can be dangerous and should be switched off when putting articles in and out. A kiln with automatic heat control is the most desirable.

LIVER OF SULPHUR: Sulphurate potash bought from the chemist in lump form and dissolved in boiling water (pea-sized lump to ½ gallon water) — used for oxidizing copper, preferably by dipping. Superseded by Coppertone which is simpler to use and gives better colours.

MANDRELL: A tapered metal form used in a bench vice, to hammer the shape (using a hide mallet) into a ring or bracelet. (For a bracelet a 5 cm diameter dowel can be substituted.)

OIL OF LAVENDER: Use as an adhesive when enamelling copper as an alternative to Gum Trag. Allow to dry before firing or the fumes will ignite and spoil the job.

OXIDIZING: Darkening copper by use of Coppertone, Liver of Sulphur or just by leaving exposed to the air. Finger prints will leave oxidized spots on a piece of copper if handled after polishing before being sealed with lacquer.

PANEL PINS: Fine nails with small heads used for string designs. Also used for securing pictures into frames.

PICKLE: Used to clean copper, especially to remove fire scale after annealing, or firing enamel. Concentrated sulphuric or nitric acid diluted with water (100g/l), in a glass or plastic container. Use copper or wooden tongs to handle articles and rinse well in running water.

PLANISHING: Polishing copper by beating on a metal stake with a highly polished ball pein hammer. Used on bowls, plates, etc. Shape is refined at the same time.

PLIQUE-A-JOUR: Is a method of enamelling where holes in the metal are filled with transparent enamel so that light shines through like a miniature stained glass window. For small holes damp enamel powder is held in by capillary action, larger ones must be worked on a sheet of mica which is peeled away when cool. Coiled shapes in copper wire can also be used for this method. Clean off fire scale in Sparex 2 or pickle.

SGRAFFITO: A design made by scratching through a layer of paint to expose a different colour underneath. Very effective in enamelling where a layer of base colour is fired, covered with a dusting of contrasting enamel powder and before firing a pattern is scratched through with a sharp point, a match stick or an eraser depending on thickness of the line desired. When fired the base colour shows as a pattern against the background of the second colour.

SILVER-SOLDER: Strong solder, best for edge joints, high melting point approximately 618-835°C depending on kind.

SOFT-SOLDER: Solder with a low melting point approximately 185-216°C. Suitable for attaching findings or for joining two flat faces e.g. a brass shape to a copper pendant. Not good for edge joints.

STAKE: Highly polished steel or hardwood shape on a shaft which is securely held in a vice or special hole in a workbench used in conjunction with polished ball pein hammer to finally shape and planish a beaten article such as a bowl.

STOP-OUT VARNISH: Paint which protects the metal from action of acid when etching e.g. Asphaltum paint.

TRIVET: Triangle of metal with points bent up to support a counter-enamelled piece. Can be bought in set of 4 sizes small to big, for pendants to plates.

'WET AND DRY': Silicone carbide paper available in very fine grades is a hard abrasive which can be used wet or dry to clean and polish copper surfaces. Begin with 400, then 500 and finish off with the finest, 600. Best used in long strokes rather than in a circular motion to achieve a smooth finish.

WIRE MESH: Used when enamelling, to support pieces, either flat on a tripod for a gas torch, or bent for use in a kiln. Heavy grade stainless steel mesh is dearer but longer lasting.

WORK-HARDENED: Metal becomes hard when beaten. Soften by annealing then clean in pickle and continue until hard again. This process can be continued until the desired shape is achieved.

Index

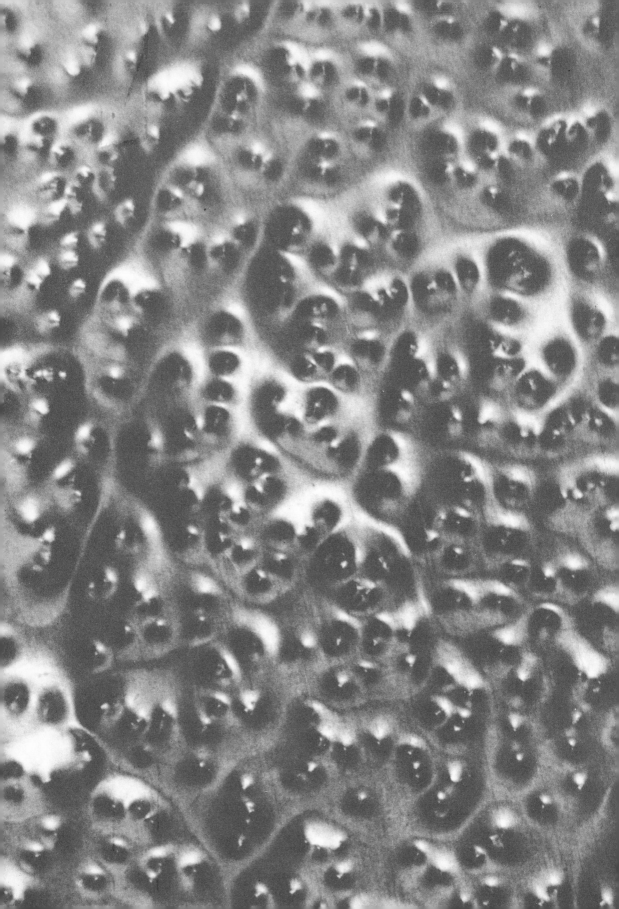